FOR HIS GLORY

*Your life may be the only Bible that
some people ever read.... So live it well !*

WRITTEN BY, REV. MAX L. MANNING

Exulon ELITE

For His Glory
Your life may be the only Bible that some people ever read.... So live it well !
Written by, Rev. Max L. Manning

Printed in the United States of America

ISBN 9781498425933

Scripture quotations taken from the King James Version (KJV) – public domain

www.xulonpress.com

Table of Contents

Meet The Parents of, Rev. Max L. Manning

Mr. & Mrs. William and Alpha Manning engaged for sixty two years of a wonderful marriage union before they graduated to Heaven.

INTRODUCTION

———⚬⚬⚬———

"Remember his marvellous works that he hath done…"
I Chronicles 16:12

It was around February in 1961, and Opal Mullin lay critically ill at St. Margaret's Mercy Hospital in Fredonia, Kansas. She had been diagnosed with cancer in the worst stage, as well as a serious heart condition. Her doctors really didn't think they could save her life, but were going to perform a drastic surgery in a desperate attempt to do so. Understandably shaken, she had asked her sister to contact a certain minister she knew of to come and pray for her. She had never met this minister in person, but was acquainted with him by way of his daily radio broadcast.

The evening before her surgery was to take place, this quiet man of God entered her room unannounced. As Mrs. Mullin looked up to behold his face, she appeared startled, her eyes widening as if in astonishment for the moment. Her visitor softly said, "I have come to pray for you," and without delay, he did just that. He then left as quietly as he had come. To the doctors' utter amazement and to everyone's great delight, Mrs. Mullin was miraculously and completely healed. Surgery was no longer required and she was released from the hospital the very next day.

The man of God who had been summoned was the Rev. Max Manning of Topeka, Kansas. Faithful to the call of God and to the cry of a soul in need, he had gone that evening to pray over Mrs. Mullin. Rev. Manning was to learn later that in addition to the wonderful physical healing that had taken place, something else truly miraculous had occurred. From the time he had entered the hospital room that evening, Mrs. Mullin had seen only the face of Jesus, and never his. Her eyes had been anointed to behold her beloved Savior, and it was Jesus who had laid His hand upon her head and imparted divine healing. Brother Manning was completely hidden behind His glory.

This is just one of the many true-life experiences that has endeared the Rev. Max Manning and his precious wife, Mary, to me in the relatively short time I have had their acquaintance. Their stories have been a source of inspiration and encouragement, all to the glory of God, for as long as I have known them.

I am simply a pen-in-hand and will remain unsigned as the inspiring tales of their work for Jesus are laid out in the forthcoming chapters. From this point forward their stories will be told in the first person by Brother Manning himself, and as you journey with him through various hardships, labors, trials and triumphs, I have no doubt that you, too, will see Jesus.

CHAPTER 1

A CHILDHOOD OF WONDERS

"Behold, I will do a new thing..." Isaiah 43:19

Mom and Dad's Wedding Day

*M*y father was William Henry Gaddison Manning, born June 10,1891 in Squires, Missouri in the Ozarks. My mother's maiden name was Alpha Mae Hardcastle, born in Bentonville, Arkansas on the twenty third day of December in 1899. Her father was a businessman operating a small grocery store, and a farmer. My father farmed in Missouri as well. Actually, most everyone in those days were called farmers because they lived on farms. My mother's family consisted mostly of devout people some of who were preachers, and on my father's side, they were basically hard working farm people.

Mother and dad met when the Hardcastles moved to Squires, which is about eight miles outside the county seat. They were married on November 16, 1915. If you do the math, you can see that Mother was quite young, but she was mature for her age. Her mother had died at the age of thirty-seven years when she was just seven years old, so she had to take on the responsibilities of keeping house and helping to raise her siblings. She was of fair complexion and very beautiful. Dad was one-eighth Cherokee Indian. You could see the Indian in his hair, which remained black until he passed away at the age of 85. Mom and Dad were married for sixty-two years before Dad's passing on June 8—just two days before his birthday, in 1977.

From their union came ten children, six girls and four boys. I was their seventh, born on July 27th, 1928. We had a wonderful, loving family with strict discipline. Mother was like a British drill sergeant, very stern, yet loving. She had a way of just looking at us and we knew we'd better straighten up and act right. Mother would never allow a deck of cards, a cigarette or an alcoholic beverage in the home, and she had very little tolerance for people that abused their bodies with such habits. She was very strict with us, giving us direction in the kind of life we should live.

When I was still very small, my mother became concerned about my dad's behavior. He co-owned a tomato canning factory, a farm and a sawmill, and a lot of his friends and acquaintances were moonshiners. Dad would be involved with them and would on occasion come home with liquor on his breath. Mother just could not take this, and she pulled a great bluff on Dad, announcing that she did not

**Uncle Thomas Jefferson "Dick" Hardcastle moved
all of us from Missouri to Fredonia Kansas**

want to raise her children in that environment and she was getting out. She told him she was moving to southern Kansas, and she gave him an ultimatum: He could either come along or stay behind. She was really hoping, of course, that he would come along but she took her stand with her children's best interest in mind. Dad decided to leave all his affairs in Missouri, and so we settled in Fredonia, Kansas, when I was quite young.

After we got settled, Mother began to grow very close to the Lord. She lived a very devout life in what light of the Gospel she had. At that time, there was no Pentecostal church in our community, and we didn't even know what Pentecost was. As kids, we went to the Methodist or Presbyterian church for vacation Bible school.

A Life-Changing Event

There came a time around 1935 when there were a lot of young people dying from diseases such as polio and diphtheria. Tetanus, which was more commonly called lockjaw in that day, also claimed many lives, and several of our little friends died. There was no hospital in our community, and only two doctors, and there was little medical intervention that could be counted on.

My thirteen-year-old sister Kathryn, third-born among the siblings, became critically ill with lockjaw, and in a short time, she succumbed to the illness. I remember clearly the day she passed away: There were two doctors present, Dr. Flack and Dr. Kilpatrick. I can still see Dr. Flack's pinstriped suit in my mind's eye.

My Sister Kathryn

When Kathryn died, they pulled the sheet over her head: her eyes were set, and her jaws locked. She was physically, clinically dead, and there were no signs of life whatsoever. For two hours, the doctors stayed with our family as we wept over a young life lost.

After about two hours had gone by, five ladies, completely unknown to us, approached our home. Each wore her hair rolled up into a bun at the back of her head, and each was dressed in a very plain long-sleeved full-length dress. These ladies didn't know us, but they had somehow heard that Kathryn had expired. They asked mother's permission to pray for Kathryn, and through her tears, Mother responded, "But she's dead." We had never seen a miracle or even heard of something such as raising the dead. The ladies indicated that they had been directed by the Lord to come and they wanted to pray for Kathryn. Mother consented, not knowing that anything miraculous would actually happen.

The two doctors were still standing there, and you can just imagine what their thoughts were at the time.

Given permission to pray, these five ladies went forth boldly and laid hands on Kathryn, commanding death to leave and life to return. The Holy Ghost took them over and spoke in other tongues, though we didn't have knowledge of what it was at the time. Within thirty seconds, my sister Kathryn was back with us! As life returned to her body, healing came with it. She was made completely whole.

To say we were shocked would be an extreme understatement for we were actually startled beyond words! With the rest of us utterly speechless, Kathryn was the one to break the silence. She looked at Mother and said, "Mama, I'm hungry." This was surely understandable because she hadn't eaten for days in her illness. The doctors, along with the rest of us, were absolutely dumbfounded.

I've never seen a greater miracle than that one, and it did something for our family that is beyond explanation. Instantly we were made believers in the supernatural miracle-power of God, though we would have to learn the particulars from His Word.

Kathryn was absolutely normal and healthy after that, and from then on, the whole experience was such a sacred thing to her. One can only imagine what it was like to have been on the other side for two hours. Different family members, including myself, would ask her at times, "Do you want to share what it was like?" but it was too sacred and she would never go into it. That experience influenced the remainder of her life without a doubt. She lived faultlessly and was truly immaculate in the righteousness and holiness of God, and she raised wonderful, godly children as well. Kathryn kept the precious secrets of her wondrous journey to herself until she got to experience them again when the Lord called her back home on September 25th of 2008.

This great miracle did something not only for our family, but for the community as well. The doctors who had been there talked about it, as did the community at large. As for the five ladies whom God had led to our home to pray, when life returned to Kathryn, they simply backed away and left without so much as a word. We found out later that they were believers from an up-and-coming Pentecostal church. God had used them mightily to start us on our journey toward the light of the baptism in the Holy Ghost.

The Full Revelation

Then the great step into Pentecost came shortly after this when the Assemblies of God began their church in our community. I clearly remember their preacher, a man with very little hair who played the guitar. My oldest sister, Geneva, was fourteen at the time, and was invited by a neighbor girl to go to church. Mom and dad said okay, asking only that she be home early. Of course, everybody walked in those days.

Later that evening, we heard a lot of noise outside and it seemed to be coming in our direction. Everyone wondered what in the world the commotion was, and we soon found out it was Geneva! She

My Sister Geneva

was dancing and shouting and speaking in another language as she came down the street. The neighbor girl was trying her best to restrain her, but without much success. Mother and Dad were alerted immediately and we kids were all looking out the windows to see what was going on. Mother's first thought was, "What have they done to my daughter?!" It was something to see my oldest sister leaping for joy and praising the Lord. This was truly a new thing.

When the neighbor girl got Geneva to our door, she left her with my parents and fled, as though she had done something terribly wrong! Mom and Dad brought her inside and tried to put her in bed, but she just kept kicking the covers off while she shouted the praises of God. She was so happy and joyful, and try as they might, they couldn't bring her out of it.

Mother was determined to see what those people had done to her oldest child. Dad, who wasn't as close to the Lord at the time, encouraged Mother not to be hasty, and even suggested that maybe there was something they didn't know about. How right he was! Geneva was in this condition all night long, and couldn't go to school the next day because she was still speaking in tongues. The siblings thought it was a riot, though we couldn't make sense of it all. We'd never seen her act that way, but she was so happy that we decided it must be something good.

The church was having meetings every night because they were just getting established, so Mother went alone the next evening, and sat on the back bench. Geneva's "condition" had begun to ease, but she was still overflowing with great joy and happiness, and Mother was determined to get some answers. As the preacher came forth and began to sing, the congregation joined in, and before Mother could get fixed, her hands and arms were pulled heavenward as if by some great magnet. She was drawn toward the altar and began speaking in other language. No further explanation was needed. This was what Geneva had experienced!

Upon mother's infilling with the Holy Ghost, our church affiliation shifted to the Pentecostal church. Mother became a pioneer member of what is now First Assembly of God in Fredonia. For twenty-seven years, she was a teacher for hundreds of little boys and girls in Sunday school. She also had a home ministry where she took Bible lessons to shut-ins and others who could not come to the house of God. Mother had a desire for the gifts of healing so she could help the sick in the community. As far as I know, she was never given that specific gift, but she did pray for many who were definitely healed. As a child, I remember hearing Mother give messages in tongues, or an interpretation, or a word of prophecy, and it always made my hair stand up to hear God in her voice as it went forth.

The Spirit of God moved in unbelievable ways back then. At that time, the church had an old pot-bellied wood stove right in the middle of the sanctuary for heat in the winter. The fire would be so hot at times that the black stove would turn red under its intensity. Mother would shout and dance in the Spirit unashamedly, and on two separate occasions, I witnessed her fall under the power of God right over that red-hot stove. She received absolutely no harm and no ill-effect whatsoever; not a hair was singed, and there was not a single burn on her body or her clothing. As I witnessed those incidents, I remember being truly awe-stricken! That was very supernatural, akin to the miraculous story of the three Hebrew boys that I had learned about in Sunday school. There before me the Bible came to life.

These were the types of things I saw in my growing up in the lives of my Spirit-filled mother and siblings. Several of the kids became involved in full-time ministry, and some are in ministry yet today. None of my six sisters ever got into trouble or went into sin. They served the Lord from childhood and received the Holy Ghost at very young ages. In fact, our entire family was saved and baptized in the Holy Ghost in their youth, with the exception of me. Growing up, I thought it was all wonderful, good and right, but the Holy Spirit never dealt with me on an individual basis. That was to come a bit later.

CHAPTER 2

COMING OF AGE

"This is my beloved, and this is my friend. "
Song of Solomon 5:16

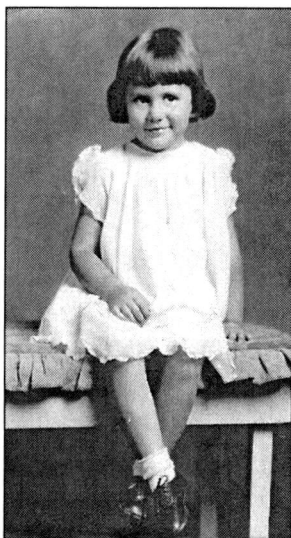

Mary, a cute little girl

*M*y precious helpmate of more than sixty seven years was born Mary Audine Smith on July 8, 1929, in Udall, Kansas. Her parents were lifetime farmers who had lived in Colorado until just before she was born. In

1943, they sold their farm and moved just nine miles away from us to Altoona, Kansas.

All Mary had ever really known was farm life, but now she found it necessary to come into town to go to school. As the good Lord would have it, our paths were soon to cross. I was working in a supermarket at the time, back at the meat counter, and in she walked one day, the most beautiful girl I had ever seen. Mary declares it was love at first sight, and to this I wage no argument.

Rather than making the trip home every day after school, Mary decided she needed a place to stay in town. My oldest sister, Geneva, invited her to stay in her home, and Mary would help with the housekeeping and caring for the children. This arrangement worked out wonderfully for all parties, and it meant that I would get to see Mary more often, something I never complained about. She would come into the supermarket at different times, and we started dating in late 1943.

A Time Of Separation

By 1945, World War II was winding down, and I felt a strong desire to join the armed forces. I enlisted with the U.S. Marine Corps in the summer of that year. By this time, Mary and I were very much in love, and with my departure for the service drawing near, I knew we needed to make our commitment to one another firm. So in September, while sitting with Mary in front of a JC Penney store, palms sweating and heartbeat at double cadence, I finally managed to ask the all-important question. To my delight (and relief) Mary happily accepted. Our commitment was solid as God was our witness, and knowing this carried us through the next couple of years during which we would be apart.

**Mary and Max on their
wedding day**

I went away to boot camp that December. Throughout our time of separation, Mary and I communicated by letter, each one a treasured token of our hearts. No two years has ever seemed longer, but finally, I got to come home. I was actually released a little early due to the fact that I had not taken any leave, so I arrived home in November of 1947. Mary and I decided to get married right away, that very month in fact, on the 27th.

Thus began what has now been more than six decades of true friendship and happiness in marriage as the Lord planned between husband and wife.

We Wrestled Against Flesh And Blood

As a child, I remember often engaging in wrestling matches with my brothers. Then growing into a young man, I always had a strong desire to fight, and most of the time it was bare-knuckle. As a teenager, every Saturday night, my friends and I, probably twenty or more of us, would go out of town where we would be equally matched with about twenty farm boys from New Albany, Kansas. Everyone knew we were there to fight—and we did actually hurt one another during these hand-to-hand combats. We would all stand facing each other, just waiting for someone to strike the first blow, and then everyone would break out fighting. We always feared that someone might call the police, but somehow we managed to avoid any legal entanglement.

One particular night, I struck the first blow, and then both sides exploded as usual. I had my opponent down on the ground and was getting the better of him, when all of a sudden his father comes up from behind and starts beating me across the back with a cane. I ditched the competition that night and got away from him as quick as I could. I was no match for an angry papa with a walking stick!

The fellows always called me an instigator, and I guess I carried that into the Marines. I went into boxing quite regularly, and we had boxing competitions as part of our recreation.

You *Will* Reap What You Sow

Being an instigator; I was also given to having fun at other people's expense. In our first home right after we were married, just before bedtime I decided to set a chair on edge and tie a string from the chair to the bedroom. I tripped it after we went to bed and it sounded like someone was breaking in. It startled Mary half to death, and oh, I thought it was great fun at the time.

Later then, a better house opened up for us three doors down and we decided to move. As we packed our boxes, I would set the ones we were finished with out on the lawn. It never crossed my mind that something might get into the boxes as they sat out there. One night after moving in, I felt something pass over my legs, and I laughed to myself smugly because I just knew that Mary was trying to get me back for the trick I had played on her. But the next day, Mary was in the kitchen, and she looked over toward the screen door and saw a snake trying to make his exit! Suffice it to say that I thought twice about pulling practical jokes after that.

Mama'sPrayers

When the Korean War broke out in 1950, I was the first Marine out of Kansas to be called back to duty. I had 24 hours to get to the west coast where I would go through rapid training before being sent to the battlefield. I had three security numbers at that time, one of which was *Special Security.*

After a hurried training period, 5,000 men, myself included, found ourselves boarding a ship in San Diego to go directly to the war front in Korea. Suddenly an officer appeared with a bullhorn commanding our attention. He asked, "Is there any man among you with a *Special Security* number?" I didn't respond for the moment because I had it set in my mind already that we were going to the war front into battle. It was obvious that we were all geared up for it. The officer repeated his question, and with this I raised my hand. He said, "I need you. You are going to San Francisco. You will have to be on the train within the hour," and he advised me that he would take care of my medical and personal records.

I did not know it at the time, but my Spirit-filled mother had prayed the prayer of faith for me. We're told in James that the effectual fervent prayer of a righteous person availeth much, and Mother's prayer kept her unsaved son away from the front lines of the battle. Surely God had a reason for sparing me from the war front and quite possibly sparing my life, but I would not know all about it until some years after that.

Chapter 3

COMPLETELY TRANSFORMED

—⸙—

*"And that ye put on the new man, which after God is
created in righteousness and true holiness."*
Ephesians 4:24

In May of 1952, I was honorably released from eight
years of military service, and Mary and I didn't
really know what to do with our lives or what direction
we were going to take. My brother Gearl was pastoring at
Williamstown, Kansas, and he invited us to church, an invitation that would turn out to be the best of my entire life, though
I didn't think so at the time. I believe it had been thirteen
years since I had last seen the inside of a church.

When Gearl spoke to us about coming to service,
admittedly I did begin to feel some small concern about my
spiritual condition, but for some reason, I just didn't want
to go to church yet. Mary was a Presbyterian, a person of
high-moral standards, but she had never been born again
either. I began to think about my brother's life, how he had
been a pastor for many years, and I really began to feel like I
didn't want to disappoint him. As if he had read my thoughts,
he sent me a card through the mail, and the essence of the
message was, "If you prepared a nice meal, and you invited
guests, and they didn't come, how disappointed you would

be." The implication was clear, so I said to Mary, somewhat reluctantly, "Okay, let's go."

We went to Gearl's church the very next Sunday morning, and the Holy Spirit began to deal with my heart immediately. The Word describes this kind of dealing in John 16:8: "And when he is come, he will reprove the world of sin, and of righteousness, and of judgment." Despite having grown up in a home that embraced Pentecost and the fullness of the Gospel, this was the first time the Spirit had ever clearly brought conviction upon me. For the first time, I was feeling the weight of my sins and the great impact of real Holy Ghost conviction. I didn't know much about the Word of God in a personal way, only what I had seen in my family's lives, but I knew that I would have to experience something very fantastic to be delivered from the great burden I was feeling. When the altar invitation was given and the people began to sing "Just As I Am," Mary and I went forward hand-in-hand, weeping with godly sorrow. We were both gloriously saved that morning.

Our coming to the Lord sparked a great revival in the church. I suppose our being so young played a part in this, and many young would follow our footsteps to the altar. In the coming days, forty-five more people were gloriously ushered into the Kingdom, and many of those very same individuals are in the ministry yet today. The church had a pond, which was very handy indeed, and so several of us new converts quickly followed the Lord in water baptism.

Power For Service

Next we needed to be baptized in the Holy Ghost — an absolute must for all true believers — but it was here that I met with a great deal of difficulty, not on the Lord's part, but on mine. I had a fair amount of reserve in my nature, no doubt due to my military discipline. My training was to "never give

23

myself over to a stranger," and this mindset evidently carried over into my civilian life. Unwittingly, I viewed the Holy Spirit as a stranger. I knew He was a person, and I knew He wanted to come in to dwell; but to give myself over was difficult because I knew it would take me out of the driver's seat. So what was meant to be a simple yielding to receive instead became a great struggle to obtain.

At the altar, the saints of God would encourage me and try to give me appropriate instructions, but all to no avail. On my mind were some of the experiences my brothers and sisters had had when they were baptized in the Holy Spirit. Some had seen a great light that came closer and closer until it finally enveloped them and they were baptized and began to speak in other tongues. So at first, I looked for a light, too, but it never came. God deals with each of us individually and His methods can be quite different at times. God is not a man and His ways are definitely past finding out.

A big hindrance to my seeking for the Holy Spirit was the fact that I had spiritual pride and didn't realize it. God tells us in His Word, "Those that walk in pride he is able to abase," (Daniel 4:37), and I was soon to find out the reality of this truth. Reality would come partly through an old farm lady named Sister Kalie.

My brother's church was in a farming community of wonderful, godly people, and in her old print dress, Sister Kalie was, in appearance, straight off the farm. I guess she saw me struggling to receive the Holy Spirit and became determined that I pray through. Here begins the aforementioned abasing: As I was on one side of the altar, she approached me from the opposite side and locked her fingers on each of my hands in an Indian deathgrip! Here I was, dressed in a fine suit, my hair the jet black of youth, looking very smart indeed, and I was being held captive by a little old farm lady. As if that weren't enough, dear Sister Kalie must have made her dinner that evening an entire plate of green onions. I love onions, mind you, but certainly not second-hand!

Sister Kalie declared, "Brother Max, we're not leaving here until we have the Holy Ghost!" and she said the easiest way to receive Him was to just start worshipping Jesus and to keep your mind on Him. Under the circumstances, that was easier said than done! She worshiped the Lord with me, and every time she hollered *Glory!* all those onions hollered with her! Oh Lord, it was awful. What I didn't realize then was that God in His graciousness was dispelling the pride in me. I was becoming thoroughly humiliated, and to tell you the truth, I think I nearly died!

Just when I thought it couldn't get any worse, the final blow landed—literally. Always in the month of May we would have scores of large bugs in that area, and promptly at six o'clock, my bug arrived. Perhaps a little disoriented and obviously off-course, he decided to crash-land in my open mouth. The Bible says that God inhabits the praises of His people, but I don't remember reading anywhere that insects will do the same! To my utter dismay, this unwelcome visitor became lodged in my throat; he wouldn't go down and he wouldn't come up. And about this time, Sister Kalie intensified her efforts. Max Manning was now completely humbled, face down in the dust as if it were.

Self now dethroned, I began to praise the Lord with all my heart and I fell under His mighty power. I laid there, the Holy Ghost witnessing through me in other tongues, for almost five hours. A person sitting close by numbered sixteen different dialects, each very distinct, that the Holy Ghost spoke during that time. I felt so glorious and wonderful that I didn't want to get up; I didn't even want to move. I just wanted to stay on the floor in His presence.

At the same time I was receiving my baptism, Mary was blessed with the holy laughter of the Spirit at the other end of the altar. What a special blessing that we received the Holy

Ghost at the same time. Mary had a group of ladies around her, and with the exception of Sister Kalie, a group of men was gathered around me. Everyone was so excited at what we'd received, and we were so weak under the anointing that they had to carry us home that night. Nothing mattered, only Him.

The forty-five people mentioned earlier that were saved as a result of our coming to the Lord were also baptized in the Holy Ghost. Revival fires had been ignited, and it was a real outpouring of the Spirit!

The first year or two of my Christian walk, I cried continuously in brokenness. The tears were from the Holy Spirit, but I did not fully understand this. God was breaking up fallow ground. I could not testify, or pray, or even pray for others without crying. When I began to cry, other people would begin to cry, too. In my prayer closet, I would pray for God to take the tears away and ask Him to make me like other people. I wanted to be able to express myself like they did. I felt inferior and ashamed because I wasn't like others, nor was I what I thought I should be. But the reality was, in fact, that I was so effective for the Lord when I allowed him to weep through me. The Lord did take the tears away eventually, and later I came to learn that God had made me that way.

CHAPTER 4

CALLED TO THE LORD'S SERVICE

---·——❧——·---

"Who hath saved us, and called us with an holy calling,
not according to our works, but according to his own
purpose and grace."
II Timothy 1:9

pon being saved and filled with the Spirit, I felt such an urgency to get the Gospel out. Everyone must have an opportunity to receive what I had received! I would go on the streets every day and witness, giving out tracts and leading people to Christ. I felt such an overwhelming urgency, and I felt the call of God so heavy upon me. I didn't feel I would qualify to enter a theological seminary, and I wasn't sure I had time anyway. I thought the Lord was coming right away, and whatever I was to do in life, I wanted to get right at it.

My brother Gearl was my mentor, along with my precious mother. In addition to being a pastor, Gearl was manager for Sears Roebuck. The company had seen in me potential to follow in Gearl 's footsteps. I began to work for Sears and they immediately made me a department manager over soft lines. I worked there for a short time, but then came a day when the call of God was so heavy upon me and I was just literally intoxicated with the Spirit. I walked off the job and continued walking five miles to our home. The Spirit of God was on me so, I had completely forgotten about my car. When I arrived home, I fell on the living room floor and began a period of fasting and prayer right then. I must get this matter resolved! There's really no way to adequately explain how you feel when the call of God is upon you like this: You know you're called, yet you feel inadequate, and you know that God must confirm it to you beyond a doubt and then equip you for the task. The whole thing was beyond me and I needed a supernatural confirmation from the Lord.

As I tarried before the Lord, the family went and brought the car home. When I left my job at Sears, I knew that was the end. It was, "Woe is me if I don't preach!" and yet at the same time, "How can I preach unless He shows me that He can give me divine equipment?" I laid on the floor of the living room for eighteen days, taking only water. Mary joined me in prayer and some fasting as well, but this was a matter that was between me and God. On the eighteenth day, I said, "Lord, you've got to speak to me. I know I'm called, but I don't feel adequate. I don't feel I can stand before people and express myself." After that, what I had been looking for finally came: God spoke to me audibly and He told me to arise. He said, "I have called you with a holy calling." He went on to say that He was going to bless me, and wherever I appeared in ministry, there would be a great appreciation for the wisdom and the words that I would bring. He told me I was going into all the world. At that time, I couldn't even imagine such a thing!

The Lord then said that His gifts and calling are without repentance, and at this I remember saying, "Lord, I don't know your Word. What does that mean?" He replied, "When I call someone to the ministry, I don't change my mind about it." Now I was truly able to rise up with the assurance in my heart that I would be a minister — that I *could* be a minister — because God had said so.

In The Beginning

I knew that Mary and I must go to work for the Lord immediately. Alongside another brother in Christ, my first act of ministry was to help establish the Topeka Rescue Mission. In the early days, I would go to the mission in the mornings to share the Word of God and to pray with the people. From this humble beginning, today the mission has expanded into a multi-million dollar operation, consisting of numerous large buildings.

Then Mary and I went to a place called Valley Falls, Kansas, which was a Catholic community. We rented a store building to hold services in, and up to this time, I hadn't preached an actual sermon. I didn't even know how to get a sermon together. In those days preachers would come into a community and put out their flyers advertising the healing ministry and all of that, so I copied the standard protocol, put my picture on a flyer, and advertised Valley Falls' "newest church." I didn't have credentials with anyone, but since my mother and brother were both affiliated with the Assemblies of God, I decided to call the new church Calvary Assembly. At that time, I didn't know the importance of "credentials." I only knew that God had called me, and to me that seemed more than sufficient.

Also on this flyer were these words: "Come and hear this young and challenging man preach the Gospel." Those words haunted me for the next several days because I had no idea how to prepare a sermon! I knew nothing at all about it, and I didn't want to ask my pastor brother. I wanted God's calling to prove itself real.

On Sunday morning, twenty-eight Catholic individuals, lovely people, came to that storefront service. My wife, Mary, had played instruments and sang all her life, so naturally she was my music. Joyfully she sat at the old upright piano. Starting time was drawing near, and the devil was really playing a number in my mind because I still didn't have a sermon, yet I had advertised myself as "young and challenging." As I stood there, I must admit, my legs were really shaking. Suddenly the Lord dropped a thought into my heart: Abraham was a pioneer. I took that thought and began to preach about how he left his homeland, not knowing where he was going. I told the people that it was much the same with me, that I had come not knowing anyone in the community, but I was there to establish a church and do a work for God. I told them with candid frankness that I was a beginner, but I assured them of my sincerity and trueness of heart. I remember saying (and I laugh as I write it now), "If you'll bear with me, we'll have a true work of God."

When I gave the altar invitation that morning, all twenty-eight individuals came forward and were saved. Praise God! I can hardly express how exciting it was to see results like that in my very first service. That was the beginning of our calling and the beginning of the work in Valley Falls. We were on our way with the Lord!

The following Sunday night, something truly amazing happened. The storefront church filled up completely. There must have been 200 people present. As I stood before the people, I expressed to them my feeling that something unusual was going to happen. I acknowledged that I did not know all the ways of the Spirit, but there was an unusualness there that night, to the point we felt almost afraid to move because of the thickness of the presence of God.

Mary had gathered about thirty small children on the stage to get them organized into a little choir, when suddenly the Spirit of God began to move and every one of those children fell backward under His power. When this happened, two children standing near the altar were instantly baptized in the

Holy Ghost, and they began to prophesy in word and in song. It was beautiful and awe-inspiring how they glorified the Lord, and it was causing great excitement among the crowd.

Some folks there that night had never witnessed anything like this before, but this was only the beginning of God's move. As the Spirit continued to sweep the place, a sixteen-year-old girl suddenly let out a great cry and fell under the power in the center aisle. For modesty, we covered her with a bedsheet that was conveniently nearby. At about this time, two women in their eighties who lived above the store rushed downstairs to investigate all the commotion. When they opened the doors and took in what was going on inside, I remember hearing one of them say, "My God! One of them is dead!"

This move of God began to attract the attention of the public. To be honest, I sat on the stage petrified; I really didn't know what to do or say. Someone said, "We'd better call the county sheriff," and another person went off to do just that. Riveted with fear, I told the Lord that I didn't know what to do. Then with wonderful reassurance, He impressed upon my heart that I was not the one who started this and that I was to just stand still. The Lord was the Master Conducter and He was orchestrating everything that was going on. I was just to sit there and be an observer. My darling Mary just played and sang during that whole time.

As I watched from my seat, the young people began to come to and were being baptized in the Holy Ghost. The young girl got up from under the sheet — quite alive and quite well — and then all kinds of manifestations and healings began to take place in the audience. Soon the doorway was literally jammed with people. At one point there were maybe twenty or thirty heads peering inside, and later I would find out why.

In addition to the mighty manifestations that were taking place in the storefront service, another truly miraculous event was happening across the street in the local theater. When the power of God began to move so mightily, a message in tongues went forth, and somehow the interpretation of the message was given over the audio system in the theater! The message warned the people to get ready for the Lord was soon coming. The theater was a good 200 feet away from our service, but all the people inside heard the message. Clearly shaken, the people vacated the theater and jammed the front of our storefront church. The sheriff who was called refused to come, so someone tried to get the sheriff from the neighboring county of Oskaloosa, but he wouldn't come either. God knows how to do things.

The Flock Grew

The church was born in the fire of this great outpouring. So many things happened there that night that I could not possibly innumerate them all here. The Catholic community had never seen anything like that. Several families found the Lord and became members of the church as a result of that service.

Among those new members were Albert Midland and his family. Albert and his children were there that night, and shortly afterward, Albert invited me to his home. His wife had been bedfast for eight years, given up to die with a heart condition, and they had tried everything to receive her healing. They had been praying earnestly for God to visit their community and they felt that I was the answer to that prayer. I have found that is often the way things happen in one's ministry: Someone has already been praying for it to happen, and you're just fulfilling your part.

I went to the Midland home, still quite a baby Christian, young in the Lord as well as young in years. Mrs. Midland was a godly lady who had been to Bible school. She and her husband wanted to work for God, but she had been stricken with a bad heart. When I approached her bed, she was just glowing. She was an old-time Pentecostal. She told me she was so glad that God had led me there. I responded that I was just a beginner, and I proceeded to further put myself down. She began quoting scripture after scripture on healing. I quickly saw that she knew far more scriptures than I did, and within myself I wondered how I could help her.

Suddenly, the Spirit moved upon me and I instructed her to stop quoting the Scriptures and start acting on them. I told her I was going to pray for her and then she was going to act out her faith. Ever since I was baptized in the Holy Ghost, I have always felt His power strong in my left hand and arm. So I prayed and laid a hand on Mrs. Midland, and she jumped up and began dancing around. It was an absolute miracle! She was no longer sick and by no means bedridden. The Midlands went into ministry and assisted Mary and me for many years. Some of their children are involved in ministry yet today.

I preached for a year in the rented store, doing all the things a minister does from marrying to burying, and then one day someone said to me, "You should be ordained." I thought that was a rather strange comment because I *had* been ordained, and I knew just when and where it had happened: on the floor of my living room during those days of fasting and prayer. God Himself had ordained me! Was that not enough? But this party insisted, "You need to have credentials, and you need to have hands laid upon you and a charge given to you." As young as I was in the Lord, I really didn't know much about that sort of thing, but I decided if that was what I needed to do, then I was willing. So shortly after that, I became ordained with the Assemblies of God.

A Shocking Revelation

One time I was holding a tent revival in Carbondale and Scranton Kansas. We obtained a military generator for the lights and sound system, and while I did have a lapel-microphone, it was connected to a cord that ran all the way to the PA system. We did not have wireless in those days. A friend named Bill Hendrix was assisting me with the sound in that revival, and on this one particular day it had rained a lot. I preached very intensely that evening and had perspired a lot as well. I exhorted the people how they needed to release their faith. Later that evening, I called the healing line and the first person I prayed for was a 23-year-old lady from the Methodist church. As I reached out to touch her, I saw fire jump from my fingers into her forehead. Then it happened to the next lady the same way! I was still new in ministry, and I wondered if I was getting a new power. I had no idea that in reality I was acting as a human conduit between the people and the PA system. My friend Bill was getting quite a kick out of it because he knew what was going on. I guess five or six people went through the line before I finally realized that there was more than faith being released as I touched the people! I am sure you can agree it was a shocking revelation.

CHAPTER **5**

NO DEFEAT IN CHRIST JESUS

---

*"But thanks be to God, which giveth us the victory
through our Lord Jesus Christ."*
I Corinthians 15:57

*I*n May of 1964, Mary and I closed a month-long crusade in Texarkana, Arkansas, with Pastor Dial. We left after the Sunday evening service to drive to Muskogee, Oklahoma. Around midnight or 1:00, I was just quietly meditating as I drove because I thought Mary was asleep beside me. We were somewhere in Texas by that time. Suddenly, I heard an audible voice that said, "I have sought for a man." I knew it was the Lord, and I responded, "What more can I do to show you that I'm your man?" In the crusade we'd just left, I had preached twice a day for a number of days. In fact, my voice was almost gone from preaching and working the altars. The Lord continued, "I have sought for a man to stand in the gap and make up the hedge, and I could not find any." Then I asked, "Lord, *where* have you sought for a man and could not find one?" His answer was Lyndon, Kansas.

I had driven through Lyndon in the past, but I didn't know a soul there. However, the call was clear, and I told the Lord we would go and plant His work in Lyndon. That's what He said He'd been seeking. For how long, I did not know.

Unknown to me, Mary was not asleep, and she heard the entire conversation between me and the Lord. God's ways are truly past finding out. I suppose since we ministered together, the Lord knew she needed to hear the call, too. After the Lord withdrew, Mary and I talked and mutually agreed to change direction right then and set our course for Lyndon.

As we headed for our new destination, God began to give me revelation about the size and shape of the building that would be His church. It was an L-shaped structure. We stopped for a refreshment, and I drew a sketch of the building. I wrote down the dimensions it should be, showed it to Mary, and said, "This is what God wants us to do."

We continued on and came to a place called Neosho, Missouri, where they had closed an Army base. On the base was a building that looked prospective and it had a "For Sale" sign in front of it. I looked at the building and I knew I could use it to build the church. I inquired about it and when I was told the dimensions, they matched exactly what I had put on paper earlier. The owners said they would take $1,000 for the building. I asked them if they would hold a check for a day or two, and they obliged. Mary and I had no money at this time, but by faith I wrote that check.

I called a friend, Glen Broaddus, who had a trucking business and other necessary equipment, and I told him I had just purchased a building that I wanted to move to Lyndon, Kansas to start a church. He agreed to be in charge of dismantling the building and hauling it to Lyndon. We discussed his fees and I advanced him a check for $1,500. Although I had yet to secure the land for the church, I told Glen I would go on ahead to get the foundation laid and the plumbing put in, and things of that nature.

Mary and I proceeded on to Lyndon, and we came into the south part of the city. I spotted a piece of ground immediately and I told Mary that that was where God wanted us to build the church. I had a feeling the people who lived up on the hill owned the acreage we were interested in, so we drove up to try to meet the owners. They were an older couple by the name of Gray. They confirmed that they did in fact own the land near the highway. I told them I was a man of God and had come to build a church, and that their land would suit me just fine. They sold the land to me for $1,500, and immediately went into town to have the deed drawn up.

In town, I was able to locate certain members of the five-member city council. They met with me and allowed me to explain who I was and why I had come to Lyndon. I told them I had acquired the land for the church, but I needed them to give me a building permit, and I needed it that day. They asked me where I would be getting materials, and so forth, and I told them I would be purchasing much of the materials from the local lumberyard. That was welcome news to one of the committee members for he owned the lumberyard. They gave me contacts I needed for roofing and plumbing, and within the hour, the plumber and concrete man were working together to get the foundation laid. Soon Glen would be on his way with the disassembled building sections.

Miraculously, all the plans for the new church were established in just one day. I advanced checks to everyone involved, the plumber, the roofer, the electrician, and as yet, I did not have a dime. But I knew God had called and He was going to make a way.

The next morning, I went to the bank. Back in those days, a banker would often take you at face-value, which I was very thankful for. I explained how I had just come to town and wanted to build a church but I needed temporary financing. He opened an account for me and put money in it for the purpose of building the church. The building that was being brought in was like new, so we were able to use the materials as collateral. The money he put into the account was sufficient to cover all the checks I had written the day before.

Work on the foundation began and before long, Glen would be coming with the walls for the building. In the meantime, I set up a tent and advertised our meetings. With great anticipation, we arrived for service the first night, only to find that our "crowd" consisted of one little old lady. The devil began to really unleash his torture in my mind, telling me what a fool I was to try to put a church together without knowing anybody, and so forth. But I knew in my heart that everything we had done was under the leadership of the Lord.

I began to get really upset with the devil the more he talked to me. I decided to walk down to the lady and introduce myself, and when I did, I discovered that she was stone deaf. She couldn't hear a thing! I was so mad at the devil by this time that I reached down and slapped her on both ears and commanded, "Come out, you foul demons!" Instantly she received her hearing and began to cry, "I can hear!" After this, more people began to trickle in to the service. I said, "Folks, let's worship and then I want to tell you how I came to Lyndon." I piqued their interest by telling them I had some really good news for them. I wanted to make them wait a bit before I told them about the new church that was being built.

Before I spoke, a lady wanted prayer for her cataracts, which were so thick you could actually see them. I prayed a simple prayer for her eyes and then went to the front to preach. After the message, I moved down to where the people were and told them I wanted to talk. The lady I had prayed for earlier responded, "I see," and I just thought she was telling me she "understood." Her daughter saw that I was the one who did not understand, and she said, "Brother Manning, she can *see!*" God had melted her cataracts as quickly as He had opened the ears of the lady who could not hear, and He used both of these great miracles to awaken that community.

Some time later, I had a request from the Kansas Assembly of God Council to meet with their executive committee and their other officers to explain my work in Lyndon. But this was not a meeting called to necessarily encourage me or enhance my work. It was more like, "Why did you do this on your own?" type of thing. The room was filled with different officers and representatives. One person rather slyly said, "Brother Manning, we have heard that you have gone to Lyndon and you have started a work." At first I just looked at them because I knew what they were up to. I told them, "Brothers, it is true. It is not rumor," and I said that I would be glad to tell them how God had led me to Lyndon.

I decided to put the responsibility where it belonged — on God! It was He who had directed me to Lyndon to build Him a church. I returned their feigned courtesy and complimented them on the wonderful job they were doing. I said, "You presbyters, let me talk to you. I go in and plant a church, and I don't ever see you come in to wish us well." I boldly asked them, "What is the work of a presbyter?" I told them how much it would mean if they would just come around and encourage the true laborers. It was difficult to explain to them how I had accomplished all the things I had in just one day, things that would normally take five or six years. I had to conclude that it was God, all God. Having heard their fill, one of them finally said, "Well, Brother Manning, I guess that is all we need to know." I said, "Goodbye and God bless you," and that was the end of the discussion. Preachers like that *need* a good talking-to!

The Day It All Came Crashing Down

Undaunted by these religious provocateurs, I looked forward to raising the church with much anticipation. In a short time, Glen arrived in Lyndon with his 18-wheeler loaded with 2-ton sections of the building he had dismantled. It was time to fulfill the plan of God. We were going to put the church together piece by piece, so in more than one way, it would truly be an "Assembly" of God.

I had seventeen men lined up for this project, and the morning we were to start the work, and I had a strange feeling that somebody was going to get hurt. Needless to say, I felt very troubled about that. It was actually a warning from the Lord, but I did not recognize it to be that at the time.

As the sections were being unloaded, I took the most precarious position, along with Glen. We didn't have money to hire a crane, and it turned out to be more than the workers could handle on their own. They lost control of a 30-foot wide 2-ton section, and when it came loose, they screamed. I looked up in time to see that it was on its way down. When it hit me, it drove my head right between my legs and completely crushed me. It hit Glen on a part of his back, but his injuries were relatively minor. The wall got me with full force, and I was knocked temporarily unconscious.

As I began to come to, I remember the first conscious thought I had was, "Oh God, I'm crushed so badly. I can't live through this." I knew I was terribly hurt. With strength that could have only been supernatural, the men lifted the section enough to pull me out. As they did so, I was trying to tell them that I was all right and that I was trusting God. We had seen many miracles and I knew He would take care of me. What I was also thinking about was the fact that I didn't have insurance to cover medical expenses, so I was trying to trust the Lord in every way possible and delay going to the hospital. My workers were doing everything they could to help me, naturally, and they called a doctor to the scene. I continued to insist that I was okay and didn't need a doctor, but I was actually very, very hurt.

I had a friend who heard about the accident and wanted to pray for me before I got to the hospital. This friend was a preacher, very fiery and high-powered, and to him, everything was caused by "demons." In other words, if your toe hurt, it wasn't an ingrown toenail you had, it was a demon. It wasn't menopause a woman suffered from, it was a demon. So when he got to me, he grabbed my leg that was hurt the worst and began to shake it and yell, "Yea, yea, yea! Come out, thou foul spirit!" I thought, "How could anyone...! I've just been crushed under a building! I don't have a demon!" The man loved me dearly, but he really set me back, and nearly killed me..

I finally did allow them to take me to the hospital in Topeka, where my injuries were assessed. I had a total of sixty-three broken bones: All my ribs were broken in half, the small bones in my left foot and both ankles were broken, as well as both knees. Bones up around my neck were broken, and in other places as well. I also had internal injuries, which included terrible bruising to my liver and spleen. Aside from assessing the damage, there was really nothing they could do for me. I could not stand the weight of any type of cast; the pain was excruciating, and they said there was too much internal damage anyway.

The physical trauma had been so great that my hair immediately started turning gray. It was obvious from the beginning that nothing less than a miracle would bring me out of this, and I was determined to receive from God.

Reverend William Branham was in the area holding a Gospel Crusade. When he learned I had been hospitalized, he came to where I was. God gave him a vision of everything that had happened, and without anyone telling him the details, he described the whole event accurately. He said, "Brother Manning, I see where Satan tried to destroy your life and kill you, but God only allowed it to go so far." This I believed, recalling the utter helplessness of the situation as I lay beneath that 2-ton section.

Brother Branham prayed for me, and at the conclusion, he said, "You will recover completely." I was expecting to hear bones going back into place or to witness some other wonderful manifestation as he prayed, but i didn't feel a thing, nor was there any relief from the horrible pain, which was still nearly unbearable. But the Bible tells us that the just shall live by faith, and so I had to apply that one-hundred percent now.

I was released from the hospital, my feet still swollen three times their size, but I had to keep the project going. Mary and I were living in a 14-foot trailer that even for that day was not modern. On top of everything else that had transpired, poor Mary had gotten mumps on both sides. We didn't have money to take care of this, but we have always stood on the scripture where David said, "I have never seen the righteous forsaken nor his seed begging bread."

As I was pondering all that had befallen us, a precious black lady named Bernadine Goodman called on the telephone. When I picked up the receiver, she said, "Is you Reverend Max Manning?" She went on to tell me how she was stretched out before the Lord, as she called it, and He had given her my name and telephone number. She said God had dropped Mary and meI into her heart to pray for us and that we were not standing alone. This was more than music to my ears! To know that God was completely aware of us meant more than all the money in the world.

Bernadine was a great prayer warrior who spent hours and hours praying. That telephone call meant more to me than if you had put $100,000 in my hand. No price tag can be placed on knowing that God is with you and that He cares. The next morning as I left the trailer, there was a sack of groceries by the door — everything we were in need of — and in the bottom of the bag was a $20 bill. I knew the Lord was going to take care of us and that the work would indeed go on.

Initially after the accident, I was not expected to live. Later this was amended and they said I would live but I would never walk again. Again the prognosis improved: "He may walk, but he'll walk funny." The amazing thing was that in just a short time, I recovered completely, just as Brother Branham had said I would, all except for one foot. I couldn't wear a shoe on that foot because a bone was sticking up unnaturally. But in every other way I had recovered, step-by-step by faith. Finally, when it came down to the last, I laid my foot on the altar one day — literally — and I said, "Lord, you've done all the rest. Now I need you to do this," and instantly I was healed.

From the time the building fell until I was completely recovered, it was about three weeks, and all the glory goes to Jesus. Even my hair returned to it's Cherokee-black, and I suffered no lasting effects from the incident. Despite the devil's best efforts to defeat the church in Lyndon, we did get the church built. It held 200 people and still stands in that small town yet today, a tribute to the overcoming power of our God.

One interesting side story: While the church was being built in Lyndon, we held a 30-day revival in a tent. After the evening service on the final night, about 10 minutes after the last person departed, a tornado touched down right where our tent was. It destroyed the tent, but thank God for His marvelous protection and for seeing that we stayed on time with Him.

CHAPTER 6

LABORING FOR THE LORD

———⚬⚬⚬⚬———

"I must work the works of him that sent me, while it is day:
the night cometh, when no man can work."
John 9:4

*I*n 1956, Mary and I, along with John and Grace Hastings, were riding together to a storefront building where we'd opened a church in Northeastern Kansas. It was mid-week, about 6:30, and people were out on their front porches enjoying a typical summer evening. The streets were very narrow in this town, and the way people parked up and down the street didn't leave much room for through traffic. We noticed children playing in the adjacent streets as we passed through.

We were driving about 20 miles an hour, talking and preparing for the service, when suddenly, a little 4-year-old girl appeared at the front of the car. There was no time or room for evasive action. She was hit and thrown about 12 or 15 feet into the air, and then landed on the hard pavement. Even though I knew there was absolutely no way I could have avoided hitting her, it was a terrible, terrible feeling.

I stopped and got out of the car, and onlookers came running. My heart had fallen to the depths of my innermost being. Not only was I concerned for the child's well-being, but I was new in town, and I dreaded the impact something like this would have on the work. As these thoughts raced through my head, the Lord brought to my mind, "The steps of a righteous man are ordered of the Lord," and I drew from that, knowing that there had to be a divine reason this had happened. Without question, the situation was totally beyond my control.

The mother of the little girl came running, crying, "My baby! My baby!" I was pleading with God to let this be for His glory. I knew my reputation and the work was at stake. The mother swept the unconscious child off the pavement. She had a deep gash in her forehead, her clothing was torn, and it was very obvious that one of her arms was broken. The four of us followed the mother into the house, as well as the onlookers. The mother was so distraught she couldn't even think what to do. I was totally depending on God and I knew we needed a miracle. This was the most damaging thing that ever happened in my ministry. I grimaced as people identified me as the new preacher in town. The last thing I wanted to do was bring a reflection on the work of God.

That day I discovered what the gift of faith was really all about. In my heart and mind, I cried to the Lord and He graciously dropped faith, divine faith, into my heart. I took hold of the mother's arm to get her attention, and through the faith of God, I told her that her child was okay.

Everyone in the house was attentive. No one was yet tending to the child, but suddenly her bleeding stopped. She still had blood on her, but the wound on her head was closed. Her eyes opened and were perfectly straight, and the arm that had been bent backward gradually moved into its proper place. God was working an astounding miracle. The mother was absolutely dumbfounded, as were the rest of us. The little one looked at her mother and wanted to be held. She was alert and awake, and from every indication, she was completely okay.

I identified myself and explained how the accident had been totally unavoidable. I told them I was on my way to church and had to be there, but assured them that I would come back by after the service. We went to church and prayed more, still unsure how the whole thing would actually play out. When we returned to the little girl's home, she was completely all right. The family never asked for any kind of compensation because the child was okay. The power of the living God had done it!

The Lord promised in His Word that all things work together for good to those who love God and are called according to His purpose (Romans 8:28), and that was certainly proven in this incident. Rather than bringing reproach upon the ministry, the Lord was glorified as He performed this mighty miracle right before the eyes of so many.

Miracles Change Lives

Another great miracle took place while I was having a great revival in Lawrence, Kansas in 1960. Under the anointing of the Holy Spirit, I stopped in the middle of my message and addressed the pastor's wife. I said, "God is giving me a divine revelation of your body. You have had a condition from birth." The Lord gave me an X-ray-like vision and I saw the abnormalities of her digestive system. She had had to eat baby food for forty-five years because of this condition. The power of God moved and she was made whole instantly. That night after the service, she enjoyed a hamburger, greasy french fries, and a Coca-cola with no ill effects. She returned the next day and testified that her body was functioning in a normal way for the first time in her life.

Then sometime in 1965, I became acquainted with Irene Edgerton, who was an avid listener to my radio program. She requested prayer for varicose veins and God gave her a great miracle. He healed her and made her legs like those of a young woman.

God Gives A Fantastic Ability

Mary and I were eager to meet new friends in a community where we'd gone to pioneer a church, and we met two unique individuals, farm people nearing their eighties, Mr. and Mrs. Wills. Lacking the opportunity for education, the wife had never learned to read. One day she was down praying and she said, "Dear Lord, if you will help me to read, I will only read your Word. I want to be able to read the Bible." She then opened her Bible to John 3:16, looked down and read it verbatim! She began jumping up and down for joy! She didn't really know for sure if she'd read it correctly, so she ran out to her husband and asked him if she was reading it right. He confirmed that she was, and if memory serves me correctly, God's Word was in fact the only thing she was able to read. Sister Wills went all over town telling people how God had enabled her to read.

She began to pray for her husband, George, that he would receive real salvation. One morning as he was driving his tractor, a light began to shine, brighter than any he'd ever seen. He could not even see to drive the tractor. He knew his wife was praying for his salvation, so he turned off the tractor, got down and knelt before God and prayed for salvation. The light kept shining until he completely surrendered to the Lord. They were friends of ours until the Lord took them both home.

A Group Of Sisters Received Power From On High

There is a Catholic hospital in Topeka called St. Francis' Hospital, and one day in 1968, the head nun called me. She was a very sweet lady whom I had seen but never really met. She called because a Protestant family had been in a terrible accident, and she asked if I could come to the hospital. One member of the family had been killed, and the others were severely injured. I went and prayed with the family. As I prepared to leave, the nun who had called me indicated that she would be calling me again, and I assumed she was pleased that I had been able to arrive so quickly and minister to this family in need.

I was somewhat surprised when I received another call from her the very next day. She said she wanted to talk to me herself, and when I arrived at the hospital, she took me aside privately to talk. She started by saying that she knew I was Spirit-filled, and she said, "I want what you have, and I have been seeking for it." Just to be absolutely sure that I understood her correctly, I asked her if she was referring to the baptism in the Holy Ghost with the evidence of speaking in tongues. "Yes," came the reply. I asked her why she wanted Jesus to fill her with the Holy Ghost, and she responded, "So I can be a better servant and help people in times like you witnessed last night." She really felt the need of His power. Then I asked her when she wanted to receive, and she immediately replied, "Now."

It was the middle of the day in a public place, so I asked her where we would go. Conveniently, the chaplain was not in at that time, so we went to his office. I can honestly say that I have never seen anyone yield to the Lord as easily as this nun did. She was a loving person, full of God's love as well as human love, and she went through to the baptism probably the easiest I have ever witnessed. The language that came forth was simply beautiful as she worshiped and praised the Lord. It was a delight to see it take place.

When the Spirit lifted, she told me that she knew six sisters in Emporia, Kansas who all wanted the Holy Ghost, and she asked if I would go to see them. I agreed, asking only that she make the necessary arrangements. At the appointed time, I drove to Emporia, and all along the way, I had the feeling that I was getting into something a bit different than what I had experienced with the head nun in Topeka.

When I arrived, the sisters were all excited and they took me to a little chapel in the back. Before we began to pray and seek the Lord, I told them that I wanted to talk to them about the Holy Ghost because we should always be able to base every experience on the written Word. I proceeded to give them several scriptures concerning the Holy Ghost and speaking in tongues. Then I asked each of them why she wanted the Holy Ghost. Though phrased differently from woman to woman, the reason each one gave was basically the same, so she could do her work in the hospital more effectively. The first two sisters received the Holy Ghost right away, and by the end of the session, the remaining four had also received.

I must say that it was really comical to watch them go through to the Holy Ghost while handling their rosaries the entire time. I had an opportunity to tell them that the only mediator they needed was Jesus Christ, and that just as Mary had said of Jesus, "Whatsoever he says to you, do it." They agreed wholeheartedly, and I think they were pleased that I had brought Mary into the conversation.

In a separate incident, I was able to pray a Catholic priest through to the Holy Ghost after a service where I had been invited to speak.

The Greatest Work Known To Man

There is nothing greater in this life than to help a soul into the kingdom. In 1953, I was witnessing in the slum area of Topeka on 4th Street, an area teeming with alcoholics, drug addicts and prostitutes. God was really with me and helped me to win many souls. I got a call one day asking me to go over to the old Throop Hotel, a favorite hangout for the dregs of society. They caller told me there was a man there by the name of Les Squires who desperately needed God. Les was originally from the eastern part of the United States, a very educated man. To see Les in the condition I found him, one would never have guessed that he was a college graduate.

A man named Walter Wilbur went with me to the hotel as reinforcement. As we entered Les' room, our eyes fell on a man who was completely dazed, laying in his own filth and vermin. His clothes were wet with urine, and he had vomited from wall to wall. The stench was almost unbearable. I stepped up to him, introduced myself and said, "I want to be your friend." In his drunken condition, he began to curse and damn everything imaginable, and he reached up to push me away. The Lord impressed it upon me to stay with him until he sobered up so I could lead him to the Lord.

I prayed and talked with Les all afternoon and evening. All the while he spit out oaths and did everything he could to get me out of the room. Walter and I teamed up to pray for Les, desiring that he become sober and of course, that he be delivered. We were eventually joined by a third brother and continued contending for this lost soul throughout the night.

After much labor in prayer, Les suddenly became sober and gave his life to Jesus Christ. This was one of the most rewarding nights of my entire life. It was a battle all the night long, but the joy of a new-found soul gave me great strength and refreshment. I didn't feel tired at all.

Les' family came from the East and were so happy to see him in his new condition. We learned that he had left a good home and a good life. After a time, Les began to attend church, and later he met a widow lady named Anne. She was a fine lady with a home and a car, and after a period of time, they fell in love and were married. It was a joy to witness a man rise from the gutter and begin a new life in Christ Jesus. The Lord said to seek His kingdom first and He would add all the rest, and we saw that in Les: God blessed him with a job, a good wife, and he lived for Jesus the rest of his life until the Lord took him home.

Things Are Not Always What They Seem

On the lighter side, one time we were searching for new members and approached a house in the community. There was a beautiful little girl playing in the yard and she jumped on my running board. She looked to be about 4 years old. After we got out of the car, I swept the little girl up into my arms, and I jostled her in the air, and kissed her on the cheek. She was just as cute as she could be, and I told her so. Then I asked her, "How old are you, Honey?" With her reply, I felt the blood just drain from my body. She said, "I am 28 years old." I thought I was going to have a stroke!

After I got over the initial shock of this revelation, we walked into the house to meet the family. Through the windows we could see that there were two other little people in the backyard, and one "little boy" was smoking a cigar. You just never know what you'll run into when you're fishing for men!

The Pastor Didn't Tell Me.

In 1964, I was holding a revival in Grandview, Missouri. We were having a great revival despite the fact that I didn't know the people and they didn't know me. One particular night, I had a healing line, and the first person in line was a well-dressed man, quite handsome, about 35 or 40 years of age. He stood before me smiling as if I should be very proud to be praying for him. Right away I felt as though something were not right. Suddenly, the Spirit of God moved on me and I asked him, "What has happened to the love of God in your life?" His smile vanished, and he looked over at the pastor. It was obvious that he suspected the pastor of telling me about him.

What I did not know was that this fine-looking man was the head of the deacon board for the church. Nor did I know as he stood before me that he was abusive to his wife and family. He was a very selfish man, ordering steak and making his family eat potatoes. I repeated the question and said, "Sir, I don't know you from anyone else. The pastor has not told me anything about you. What I am telling you is from the Lord." The man began to scream, "My God! My God!" and he fell on his knees right there and begged for mercy.

An Unusual Ability

Many years ago, I held a crusade in Muskogee, Oklahoma, and the pastor there told us about a woman in his congregation who was quite unusual. She was an older lady who lived out in the country, and he explained that God used her in a miraculous way. As he began to tell me things about her, it gave me a great desire to meet her.

I finally had an opportunity to meet Mrs. Hobbs, and she told me that when she was a young lady, she told God that she didn't know what He wanted her to do, but that she was willing to do whatever. The Lord moved upon her hands and her eyes, and He told her that people would consult her for advice her whole life. People would seek advice and God would give answers by way of her opening her Bible and portions would stand out in flaming red.

I told her that the Lord had been dealing with Mary and me about starting a new church, and I wanted to know what God would tell her about that. She said, "Yes, you are to go." She opened her Bible and a certain scripture stood out. She said that we were to go, but that we were going to have seven years of severe trial and testing. The Lord let us know in advance that it was not going to be easy.

I had already suffered quite a bit in life, and I told Mary we had better do some praying about this. I told her to pray and ask God for a special scripture. While she prayed at home, I went to the church to pray and to seek a scripture as well. When I returned a couple hours later, we matched up our scripture and it was the exact same one, a scripture in which the Lord promised that He would be with us. We started that ministry and we did indeed go through seven years of trial and hardship. At the end of the seven years, the church was raised up strong and healthy in the Lord. It was amazing because the trials vanished as quickly as they had come.

The Lord has diversities of gifts, and people would call Mrs. Hobbs for advice from all over the world. One time she received a call from a ruler in South America, a dictator who was looking for counsel. She boldly told him that he had blood on his hands, that he was judged by the Lord and needed to get right with God.

Vengeance Belongs To The Lord

Years ago, there was a time when two families caused me much grief, hurt and trouble. I had done nothing to them, but they were just full of the devil. I did not know exactly how to pray for this situation, but as I sought the Lord, He dropped it into my heart to simply pray that they would move out of the community. I felt the assurance that they would indeed move before it actually happened. Within four days, they not only left our community, but they left the country as well. The Lord promised to do for us exceeding abundantly above what we can even think.

In 1965, we had purchased three acres in Topeka upon which to build a church. I had a sizable tent, and while the church was going up, we worshiped there. We had been having great services, and on one particular evening, for some reason, I decided not to come to the service until it was time for me to preach. When I stood and looked out over the audience, I saw a man sitting with both fists clenched and a grimace on his face. The Spirit of God gave me revelation that there were demonic spirits raging in his mind and he had evil thoughts toward me. Rather than starting my message, I addressed the man and commanded him to come forward. He came forward and stood before me, still defiant with fists clenched. No one else in the congregation knew what was going on. As he stood before me, he was cursing and blaspheming. I said, "You have come to hurt the servant of God. You have hatred against God and against His man. You must bow." Suddenly, he went out cold, as though a crane had hit him. I instructed the brothers to help lead him to the Lord. After his deliverance, he told me that he hardly even remembered coming to the meeting. I learned from his wife that he had said in the car that he was going to kill the preacher. God cleaned him up and later he became a member of our church board.

Touch Not Mine Anointed

This incident also happened in Topeka, and I will refer to this man as "John." I had been doing some work at the church, and had just arrived home. I pulled into the driveway, parked, and suddenly through the open window there were massive hands that grabbed my throat. I discovered that the hands belonged to a member of my church, John, a large, stocky man who worked for Santa Fe. Amidst the terrible cursing that was coming out of his mouth, I could hear that he was accusing me of talking about his wife and the life she had lived. He finally let up a bit, and I was able to say, "John, that's not true. I have never said anything about your wife." He would not accept this and started choking me again.

I had at least two hammers on the floor of the car, and I could have reached down and nailed him with one of them, or even thrown the car door into him, but God would not allow me to defend myself. The Lord completely disarmed me. When he let up again, I said, "John, it's best that you leave." By this time I was talking raspy because he had damaged my voice box. He reached for my throat again, and when he did, I saw a blackness go from his fingers up his arm and into the midsection of his body. When he let up for the final time, I told him that he was in trouble, that he should not have touched me, that I was not the one who had said anything about his wife. With this he raced away.

Our daughter Debbie was sitting on the front porch and saw the whole thing. When John ran away, I had to explain to her that everything she had seen was the devil working through that man. I didn't want her to be upset, nor did I want her to think that I'd done something wrong to deserve what had happened.

The very next day, I received a call from someone informing me that John was having internal bleeding. This really came as no surprise given the blackness that I had seen enter his body. At some point, John learned that it was another preacher who had talked about his wife in a prayer meeting. After he recovered from his bleeding episode, he and his wife came to church and he apologized, but I really did not feel that the apology was all that it needed to be on his part. It seemed half-hearted and lacking in sincerity. Sincere or not, I accepted his apology and left the matter between him and God.

About ten years ago, Mary was going through the VA hospital, and she heard a voice call out, "Sister Manning, I must talk to you." It was John and he was on his deathbed. He told Mary that he must talk with me, but she explained that I was in Africa at the time and wouldn't be back for a few more days. Unfortunately, John died a day before I returned home and did not get the opportunity to settle the matter, as I presume he wanted to do.

God's Mercy On Display

In June of 1970, I was pastoring Evangel Temple in Topeka, and we were hosting a crusade. It was decided that since I owned the tent, I would be the principal speaker. We opened the crusade that continued for ten consecutive nights. We had fifty-eight people saved during the crusade, which was really excellent given the size of our church.

The tent was full on the last night of the crusade, and I remember commenting to those in attendance, "In all of my ministry, this is the first time I have ever held a crusade where there was no opposition and all the bills were paid in a timely fashion." It was almost as if the devil hadn't given us any trouble at all. We rejoiced in all that God had done and in all the new souls brought into the kingdom. We would be taking down the tent and folding up the chairs, so I asked for everyone to please stay and help. With great delight, they stayed and started working.

As we were folding up the chairs, suddenly a man came leaping into the tent like something from another world, using foul language, and asking, "Where is the preacher?" I was backed up against the chairs, and when I saw the wildness in his face, I didn't know whether to say I was the preacher or not! In his right hand, he clutched a chain, and in his left, a knife. It was a rather awkward couple of seconds because I was not in a rush to introduce myself, nor did the people want to point me out and say, "There he is!"

What actually flashed through my mind was that whatever I did, it would have a tremendous effect on the new converts, and that's what made the situation that much more dire. The man started toward me, and then his wife appeared in the tent, her face scarred from previous abuse. She jumped between him and me, and she pleaded, "Bill, don't kill him! You don't even know him!" His countenance became even worse and he slashed her with the knife, cutting open one of her breasts.

Fortunately someone had called the police, and in a very short time, two officers with trained dogs arrived and took the man into custody. As they led him away, I led his wife to the Lord. I then asked her what was going on, and she said that she could not talk more but that it would be in the paper the next day. The police asked us if we wanted to file charges, and we declined to do so. However, they had enough to file on him themselves, from resisting arrest to driving with no license, so he was taken to jail.

The story did come out in the newspaper, and it was actually quite favorable toward the church. I learned that the man was Bill Tyner, and he worked as a tree trimmer, a very good one at that. That explained the agility he had displayed as he came bounding into the tent the night before. His boss had gotten him out on bail, so I decided to visit him at his home unannounced. I took one of my board members with me and I walked up to the door and right into the house. Bill and his wife had two teenage children and they fled the house immediately. I'm sure they were quite aware of what their father was capable of.

I approached Bill and said, "I want to talk with you." He began to apologize for his behavior and explained that he had been under the influence of a mixture of drugs and alcohol. I told him that I hadn't come to talk about that, but that I wanted to talk to him about Jesus, and about his soul. He then told me that he had never been in a church in all his life and there were many things he did not understand. I sat down and invited him to ask me anything he wanted. The man who had looked something akin to Legion just the night before now opened up and began to ask deep and serious questions about God. He wanted to about the origin of God, and why God would allow little children to be killed in tornadoes and earthquakes — if there was a God. I could tell that he really wanted answers to these questions, and we talked for a good two hours.

At the end of the session, I asked him if he believed. He said he had never believed before, but that he wanted to believe. He concluded that since I had shown him the truths we discussed in the Word, then it must be true. When the time was just right, I asked him if there were any reason that he could not receive Jesus right then and there, and before my eyes, a great miracle took place. He bent down on one knee, and the Lord not only saved him but baptized him in the Holy Ghost at once and he got a shouting dose! His wife was also filled with the Holy Ghost. She had been enlightened through that two hour session . His children were watching through the windows, we called them in where they were saved and filled with the Holy Spirit also.

When the Spirit lifted, Bill said, "Reverend, let's go next door." He led the way and entered the house without knocking. When the man of the house saw Bill, he jumped to his feet and took a defensive stance. He had heard the beatings next door down through the years, so I guess he didn't know what he might be in for. Bill exclaimed, "The best thing to ever happen in my life just happened. I got saved!" The neighbor man responded with, "You *needed* to get saved!"

This man was a roofer and he didn't respond to the Gospel as quickly as Bill had, but eventually he did pray the sinner's prayer. Neither us nor the man himself could have known what was to come in the next few days. His wife, a rather large woman, went out of town and dropped dead in a place of business. Her husband didn't have money for the burial, so the Lord led me to go before the church to raise money to take care of this. We gave him a big offering, and he just couldn't believe I would do that. Almost unbelievably, the very next week, this roofer-man fell sixty-some feet to his death. I really rejoiced and praised the Lord for the chain of events that led me to a soul that was so close to eternity without God. This man may have well missed heaven had I not been accosted by his devil-possessed neighbor.

Never Too Old To Change

At one time, we had a dear lady named Cora coming to the church with her daughter and grandchildren, and we were thrilled to have them among us. She was married to a ninety-year-old man who was totally against preachers, against churches, and against giving to the Lord. She told me that her husband very much resented her coming to church, and she had cautioned me to never go see him because he was very mean. I thought to myself, "How much of a threat could he be at the age of 90?" but she really pleaded with me never to go.

Cora told me one time that the little bit of money she was able to give in the offerings was money she took from his billfold without his knowledge. I told her that she must not do that any longer because that was stealing. She just wanted to give to the Lord so badly, but she assured me that she wouldn't do it that way any more. I told her to leave her man to me, and that some day, some time when it was just right, I would be knocking on their door. This actually terrified her, but I gave her the assurance that I would not go unless I was truly directed by the Lord.

Cora continued to come to all our meetings, our Bible studies and services. Her husband already despised preachers, but he developed a special disdain for me due to the fact that his wife was spending so much time at the church. He was well-aware of my work in the community and evidently knew everything about me — everything except what I looked like.

A day came when I knew the old man was at home alone, so I decided to pay him a visit. When I knocked on the door, he hollered, "Come in!" He was sitting some ways back in an easy chair, and he seemed friendly enough. I walked over and shook his hand and even gave him a little hug as I introduced myself. "I'm pleased to meet you," I said, "I'm Rev. Manning." As if I were the one hard of hearing, he said loudly, "What'd you say your name was?" I repeated myself, and when the truth of my identity dawned on him, he grabbed his cane and started hitting me with it. Cora had warned me, hadn't she? To be honest, the situation was so amusing that I could hardly stand it!

Surprisingly, the old man and I became very good friends, and I was one of the only preachers he learned to like. If having a godly mate would bring sanctification to the unsaved, he would have been assured of heaven, because his wife was truly a jewel. The kind old gentleman finally softened and gave his heart to the Lord.

In 1958, Mary and I were pastoring a church in Kansas. During a certain period of time, we had many deaths among our members. In a thirty-day period, I conducted thirty-three funerals. Many of the deceased were young people who died in accidents. One man had been electrocuted under his house. It was really something to say goodbye to so many in such a short period of time.

A Little Child Shall Lead Them

We had been bringing a precious little four year old girl named Dolly to Sunday School. Her parents were not believers and were not willing to start to church at that time. It was discovered one day that this bright, lovely child had a large tumor on her brain. She was hospitalized and the conclusion was reached that surgery was not an option. Dolly's days were numbered. Her parents were terribly broken in spirit as they realized they were going to lose their precious child.

At the hospital, Dolly looked at her mother and father, and said, "I want to sing for you." She began to sing, "Jesus Loves Me," over and over, loudly and clearly for all to hear. Then she changed the words to "Jesus Loves You," and sang it with all her heart. This broke her parents and they fell to their knees and were gloriously saved at her bedside. Two days later, Dolly passed away, still singing her beloved song.

It was a testimony to the doctors and to many other people as well. The Bible says that a little child shall lead them, and we saw this fulfilled as people came to the Lord during her funeral.

All Men Are Of Free Choice

In 1953, I knew an older lady named Mary Green, who asked me if I would visit her mother and daddy, both of whom were dying in a care home. I had led Mary to the Lord, so she had confidence in me and wanted to be sure that her parents were saved. I agreed to go and see them, and Mary met me there. She took me first to her mother, who had a crippling, deforming arthritis. Her legs were twisted and frozen behind her. She was in so much pain that she couldn't tolerate even a sheet being on her. Mary said to her mother, "My good friend, Brother Max, has come." Her mother replied, "Oh, thank you, little minister. I'm so glad you've come. I want to know Jesus." She asked me to read the 23rd Psalm before she died, and so I did. Then I prayed that Jesus would come into her life and make her His child. She had a glorious experience in the Lord. She smiled and said, "Now I am ready to go," and she died right then and there. Mary rejoiced and said, "Oh, thank God! Let's go see Daddy."

We went into his room together, and there I saw a large, military-looking individual, eyes focused straight ahead and looking very stern. She introduced me to him in the same way she had her mother, but his response was very different. Coldly he said, "Leave me alone. I don't want God." Mary said, "Daddy, I can't stand to see you not saved." She looked at me in desperation, pleading and pulling on my shirt until it actually tore. I talked with Mr. Green and tried to explain to him that he was checking out of this life that very day, and I didn't want him to depart not knowing the Lord as his Savior. He informed me that he didn't want anything to do with God, that he had told God to leave him alone and that God had in fact left him alone.

Mary cried in anguish and fell to her knees, begging her father to simply ask Jesus to forgive him. He said to his daughter for the final time, "I'm telling you, leave me alone." Deep in my heart, I felt such a heaviness, just a blank wall and a void. I knew there was nothing more that could be done. I did my best to pray for the man, but it was really just a dry, empty prayer. He had made his choice.

Mr. Green did die that day, and as he was leaving this life, he complained of heat and burning on his feet.

The Spirit Must Have Liberty

In 1956, we were invited to a particular church in Nebraska City, Nebraska, for a revival crusade. We did not know the pastor or the church, but the arrangements were made, and I called to inform them that we would arrive on Saturday. We would come in our trailer home and park it near the church. They seemed to anticipate our arrival.

When we arrived at the church, I was about to experience something I'd never experienced before. I was about to unhitch the trailer when the pastor walked up and introduced himself. He told me that he always talked with his guest speakers beforehand and said he wanted some time with me before the Sunday service. That was fine with me, but I suggested we have the talk right then before I unhitched the trailer.

The pastor was a handsome man, about thirty-five years of age. He had been a pastor at a Christian Church but was now a minister with the Assemblies Of God. As he began to tell me that he had certain rules that always applied to all guest speakers, I thought, "Oh Lord." Red flags began waving all over the place, but I let him continue. He said that he only wanted me to preach and say a prayer, and then I was to turn the service back over to him. He also advised me that he did not want his guests to greet the congregation or socialize with them in any way. With this, I told him there was no need to go any further because he had tied my hands.

He looked surprised at my response. I went on to tell him that if I couldn't bless the people, there was no need for me to stay. I told him I love people and God uses me to bless people in a very personal way. I told him I love pastors, too, and I wasn't looking to take over a church. After I delivered my heart to him, I told him that we were going to leave and head for our next crusade. He said, "Oh, you can't! I've got you advertised." I understood this, but I told him that I couldn't help him in the straitjacket he wanted to put me in. Finally, he began to compromise and loosen some of what he had said earlier. I said, "Okay, under those conditions, we will stay."

My heart went out to this pastor because it was obvious that he had a problem of some kind, though I did not immediately know what it was. He wanted a guest evangelist, but yet he really didn't. I told him I wanted to have some private time with him for prayer.

The next morning dawned, and I got a call to say that the pastor could not possibly come to church because he had gotten the mumps in the worst kind of way. We went on to the service, and I had the freedom I needed to minister to the 200 or so people in attendance. We had an old-fashioned Pentecostal camp meeting service, and several were saved and filled with the Holy Ghost. Toward the end of the service, the pastor's son, about nine or ten years of age, came to the altar weeping and God filled him with the Holy Ghost. Not only did he receive the infilling, but he was called to preach that morning. He cried unto the Lord, "Yes, Lord, I will honor you. Yes, Lord, I will serve you. Yes, Lord, I will preach for you." God moved so that the service lasted until about one o'clock.

After service, we were to go to the pastor's house so I could pray for him, and have dinner there as well. As we approached the home, I saw the pastor looking out the window like a little kid who had missed something. His wife and son came in shouting and declaring what a wonderful service we had had. The pastor tried to smile and look happy, but you could tell it was killing him.

The revival went into a second week, and by this time, the pastor was able to get into a car, so I suggested we go somewhere and talk. Many, many more good things had happened during the services, and I said, "Surely by now you know that I have come only to be a blessing." I told him that I have never asked anyone for an offering of any size at any church at any meeting (and now, more than fifty years later, I can still say the same thing). I wanted to know why he had his "talk" with all the guests who came there. He opened up to me and shared how in the Christian Church there had been a preacher who had come in to undermine him, and he had done a lot of harm. Because of that, he had built up a resistance to protect himself from that ever happening again. We prayed together, and I trust the Lord was able to help him and make the revival truly complete.

A Macedonian Call

In 1961, when I was the pastor of Glad Tidings Assemblies Of God, I received a call from five men from the Church of God seeking an appointment with me. They said that their congregation of around 300 had been fasting and praying for about thirty days. They explained that none of them knew me, but God had given them my name, and they wanted me to come and hold a crusade.

This created a somewhat of a dilemma for me because I felt that if I went to a different church, I would get reported to the Assemblies Of God authorities. The Assemblies' rules were that we were to stay within the confines of the Assemblies Of God. Yet these men were sitting there telling me that God had spoken to them and given them my name. I decided, "If God spoke to you, I will come for one Sunday and then we'll see how God directs."

We went to their church, and when we went inside, we found the people praying, and they'd been fasting for many days. There was much of the power of God in the church. Many people were saved and filled with the Holy Ghost that morning, and then again in the evening.

In light of these marvelous results, I told them that I would come back, but that first I needed to make a trip to Wichita to speak with the district superintendent. We made our appointment, drove to Wichita, and sat by a fireplace for two or three hours talking to the district supervisors. I told them all about the invitation I'd received from the Church of God, how the Lord had given them my name, and the great success we had had on Sunday. I thought surely they would see how God was moving

After sharing all of this with the authorities, I waited to hear their feelings on the matter. They informed me that my presence at the other church had in fact already been reported, and that they had to comply with the rules of the brethren. I began to weep as I did not feel this was right. I shared these feelings, though it did nothing to persuade them. With a heavy heart, I went back to the Church of God and sadly told them the situation. I explained that it was a sensitive issue, and they understood very graciously. This was not an easy thing for me as I was torn between pleasing the Lord and pleasing the powers that be. It was somewhat of a turning point in my life and was part of the reason I later made the decision not to stay in the Assemblies Of God.

Miracle On Tefft Street

In 1965, we were led of the Lord to start a new church in a certain community. We put our tent up, and in a short time we had a nice crowd of people congregating.

Next it was time to start putting up an actual building for the church. A certain lady approached me and said, "Brother Manning, I can't do the physical work, but I want to pay for the blueprints." That was such a blessing because they were going to cost about $600. This was the first of many miracles that would take place in our erecting this church for the Lord.

As we continued to develop, a certain couple joined our number who were prominent in society, and we counted it a privilege that they were a part of our fold. I trusted this gentleman one-hundred percent, and he likewise. We decided to contract this man for the building project. Normally the funds for the project would have been distributed in portions as needed, but I was traveling quite a bit to Old Mexico at that time, so I made it possible for this man, Don, to have access to all the funds.

Don was married to a woman named Margaret, and had been for over 40 years, but soon I would learn that his wife had another side. She had a habit of visiting many different ministries and making very large financial pledges to them. One day I returned from a trip and Don came to me very despondent, saying we needed to talk. He proceeded to tell me how Margaret had pledged $15,000 to a certain ministry, and had taken the money from our building account. Don felt very badly about the situation and did not know what to do.

I spoke to Margaret about the matter and her face flushed. She said she had done the deed "in the Spirit" and refused to see any wrong in what she had done. I tried to explain that it was not her money to have used in the first place. It was really a very embarrassing situation, and it brought our building project to a standstill. To further complicate matters, it was looking like it might take as much as another $30,000 to finish the project, money we no longer had.

The situation put a strain on our relationship, and Don felt that he should withdraw from the board. He had no solution to the problem, but his resignation was not going to solve anything. The only available option was to raise the funds a second time. After prayer, I carefully presented the situation to the congregation and asked, "What can we do?" The consensus was that all we could do was raise the money again and forgive. By the grace of God, we raised the money once more and got the project back on track.

We ended up with a beautiful church on a three-acre plot. Someone wrote a story about our work and called it, "The Miracle on Tefft Street." We had started building in June, and by winter we were inside the building. Indeed God had worked all kinds of miracles to make this happen.

As we finished the building, something truly sad occurred. Don, a handsome man sixty years of age, became deathly ill. Something took him over from his head to his feet; his blood vessels were hemorrhaging on the inside throughout his body. In that day, you would often see construction workers holding their nails in their mouths, and the speculation was that this may have had a poisoning effect. Whatever the cause of his condition was, Don received a sentence of death. I wanted him to know that the incident concerning the building funds was completely forgiven, and I requested a private audience with him.

When I got to the hospital, Don asked his wife to step outside. We talked, and he assured me that he was ready to go home. I did not doubt this because he was truly a prince of a guy. He told me he truly regretted what had happened, and he shared with me that all the years of his marriage had been very difficult. I assured him that our friendship was still strong and that nothing could separate it, and that there would be no lawsuit, despite the fact that the lending institution wanted to litigate. This news made him very happy and gave him the peace he needed.

Unknown to either of us, Margaret had slipped a recorder into the room. After talking with Don for some time, I turned and saw the microphone. Before I left that day, I called Margaret into the room, and God anointed me to pray like never before. I hugged Don for what would be the last time, and I hugged his wife, too, although it was not as easy. The next day, Don was in heaven. He had a huge funeral with about 800 or 900 people in attendance.

Taking To The Airwaves

Early in my ministry, I was very anxious to share the Gospel with the multitudes. I was keenly aware that faith comes by hearing the Word of God, and the Word itself asks us how they can hear without a preacher. The Lord promised to open to us an effectual door, and He has done that again and again down through the years.

In Valley Falls, Kansas, where my first church was, the local newspaper came to me and offered me the opportunity to place a daily message in their paper free of charge. It was really a blessing because I was free to write about any subject I chose. I strongly felt that I should preach about the cross more than any other subject, and sometimes I wrote as much as a quarter-page message. It was a great open door, and the newspaper continued to publish my articles for free for about two years.

At the same time, I had a strong desire to preach on the radio. I did not have any equipment at that time to produce a program, and actually, there were not that many religious radio programs in our area. Suddenly the door opened for me to go on the radio, and the amazing thing was that there was no charge for the program because it was considered a public service. The Lord provided the necessary equipment, and I was on the air in many areas, from Kansas to Missouri to Texas, all the way to the border of old Mexico.

At times I would be on as many as eight different programs a week, and often I would have a one-hour program live from the church. Other spots ranged from 15 to 30 minutes. Jesus said, "Go ye into all the world and preach the Gospel", and I was more than willing to use my voice and my talents to get His Gospel out. God has always been sovereign in the Voice of Faith broadcasts, and I have centered my ministry around Christ. I preach the cross, the power in the blood, and the Holy Ghost.

Today, the Voice of Faith radio broadcast is heard on several international stations, as well as stations in the United States. It has been a great privilege of mine to be heard on WIBW, 580 AM and and the Upper Room Radio in Topeka. WIBW Radio which is one of the most powerful stations in Kansas. The manager there approached me some years ago and said That they would like to have my program on after the news. He said that I was an icon, and they knew it would be an asset to their station to have my program on the air. Well, I didn't really know what an icon was at the time, but whatever method the Lord chose to use, I counted it as a blessing to help get His Gospel to the people. Souls are waiting to hear the good news!

My radio program is also heard in eight different countries in Africa. Additionally, I am on a station in Zambia that covers the whole of Africa, and a sister station that goes down into Australia and New Zealand. This opportunity came about through a "chance" meeting. Years ago, I was flying from Kenya to the southern part of Africa, and a man named Charles Mbaosie from Lusaka, Zambia, sat next to me. He asked about my ministry and we had a very constructive conversation. It turned out he was the general manager of the radio stations in Zambia, and he expressed an interest in airing my radio broadcast. Naturally, my first concern was the cost. This concern was immediately quelled when he informed me that it would not cost anything! He said I would be given a regular daily slot, and then would also be placed in nightly slots where there might be openings. This was truly a wonderful thing that only God could have arranged. Fifty Two consecutive years I have awakened at five AM and made preparation for my daily radio broadcast... Radio especially in the developing nations is a great soul winning tool.

Mary and I have always been so happy for this great open door, and new contacts are arising to reach even more millions with the Gospel. I did not have the resources to start this work, nor to continue it, but God has always provided miraculously. I consider one day of provision a miracle, but 52 years is truly amazing!

Taking inventory not too long ago, I numbered 10,780 different programs over a period of 52 years. The Lord has kept the door for my radio program open, and we will continue to serve the Word as long as that door stands before us.

CHAPTER 7

UNDER HIS WINGS

———⋅⋐⋙⋙⋑⋅———

"No weapon that is formed against thee shall prosper."
Isaiah 54:17

*M*any times over the years, I've had incidents occur in my life where great harm or injury would have befallen me had it not been for the ever-watchful eye of the Lord. He has covered me with His feathers time and again and protected me in ways that were undeniably Him.

In 1955, Mary and I we were traveling throughout the U.S. conducting tent meetings. I drove a 2-ton box truck containing my chairs, piano, sound equipment and so forth. Mary would follow me in our car, pulling a small trailer full of our personal belongings behind her. One day we were heading south on Highway 75 in Kansas. I was leading the way, and Mary and Glenn were behind me with full view of my truck. Suddenly, something gave way in the steering mechanism and it became uncontrollable. The truck rolled, breaking loose all our equipment, and then skidded on its side for at least forty-five feet. Watching from behind, Mary and Glenn were horrified. The truck came to a stop on its side, with the driver's door facing upward. Gasoline and oil were pouring out over the hot manifold, and the possibility of fire was very, very real at that point. Drivers who had witnessed the accident stopped their vehicles to see if they could offer assistance.

The impact of the accident tore the shoes and socks completely off my feet, and my legs felt like they were surely broken. I managed to open the sliding door of the truck and was able to lift my body up through the door. It was a good eight or ten feet down to the ground, and I knew I had to jump because the truck might explode — but how could I with legs broken? I had no other options, so I jumped and landed on both feet. Miraculously, as I hit the ground, I was healed from any damage that had been done to my feet and legs. I had no other injuries on my body, but the truck was completely totaled. We knew Satan was trying to prevent us from conducting the revival we were headed for, but there is no defeat when you are in the divine will of the Lord. We kept our schedule and started the revival on time! We were hindered, yes, but definitely not stopped. God's promises of providence and protection are marvelous indeed!

Just Call On Jesus

In 1966, our church was blessed with a large influx of Hispanic people. Among them were Maria and Felix Espinosa, both about 55 years old. Maria was really on fire for God, truly dedicated and wonderfully Spirit-filled. Felix on the other hand had not yet given his life to Jesus and was somewhat abusive towards Maria, especially when he'd been into the tequila. Maria would call me at different times, and I would pray for Felix and try to encourage him that he ought to be walking with the Lord, that He could deliver him from all of that. He knew the right way because his father was a preacher in Old Mexico.

One day a most unusual thing happened for Maria. She was a very spiritual person and she had a close connection with the Lord. She listened to what God told her, and God would move for her in great ways. On this particular day, Maria was standing in the living room with Felix, and he was about to strike her. She told him to stop immediately and reminded him of what I had told him and how he ought to be living. Boldly she warned him that if he touched her, she was going to call upon Jesus and He would take care of him Himself. Unafraid of her threat, Felix started to move toward her, and Maria raised her hand and said, "Jesus, get him!" Immediately Felix was knocked to the floor. The Lord knocked him senseless, and he got up dazed, wondering what had hit him. He started after his wife once more, and again she warned, "I'll call on my Jesus!" In a panic, he said, "No, Maria, don't call Him! I'll do whatever you say!" Thank God, after this close encounter with the Lord, Felix began to come to church and got saved.

Service In India

Many years ago, I spent some time in South India. The national religion was Hindu at that time and their constitution read that individuals seeking to influence or convert people to Christianity could be imprisoned. Converts were disowned and alienated from their families, and some were even killed by their loved ones if they gave their hearts to the Lord. During my time there, I found myself in hostile villages that were strictly Hindu, and on two separate occasions, I was approached by machete-wielding men and threatened with obvious harm if I did not leave. Both times God intervened, and I barely escaped what could have been a very bad situation.

In 1966, I was in South India, in Kerala State, preaching at different conventions and staying in different homes. For a time I was with Pastor George Varghese, a man who had great influence over the Pentecostal assemblies. This man of God was a worker and he really kept me busy. I preached three times a day for several days with him. After days and days of non-stop preaching, I was so tired that I couldn't even see straight. We came into his quarters one evening, tired, and very hungry as well. His place didn't have electricity, and they got along by candlelight. I knew Brother George really loved me and he knew how weary I was. He said, "Brother Manning, I'm going to get you a piece of bread and some honey." That sounded absolutely delightful. He brought out what looked like a fifth of whiskey in the candlelight, but it was actually a jar of honey, and I generously poured some on a piece of bread. I took a great big bite, and oh, I have to say, it was really good! Then my eyes began to come into focus, and I could see that the gooey treat I was enjoying consisted of about 10% honey and about 90% ants!

Perils In Haiti

While serving as a missionary to Haiti, I have faced many trials, difficulties and hardships in my service to the Lord and the people. I have lived through five military coups in Haiti, and during one of them, I was a witness to the worst kind of happening. There was massive bloodshed and bodies were strewn from the airport all the way to the city. I was just about to turn in one night and was sitting on the edge of my bed. I decided to lay down, and as I was looking up at the ceiling, suddenly there was a burst of gunfire that left about seven or eight bullet holes in the wall just above me. Had I still been sitting up, I would have been the one full of holes. I learned later that a Haitian colonel who was being sought by the military had been hiding just outside my door. We truly have nothing to fear when we trust in God's divine protection.

During another stay in Haiti, I had held my workers late into the night, and they needed to travel beyond Port-au-Prince to reach their homes. I owned a Polski, a small compact car, and I offered to drive them to town where they could get a taxi to take them the rest of the journey. We set off, one man, two women, and myself. We got down to the Iron Market where there is a notable "T" in the road and I pulled over next to the curb. I intended to sit there and make sure my workers got their taxi. Suddenly a large Mac truck appeared and it hit my car on the drivers side. On impact, I went airborne, and my body spun around and broke out all the windows. The driver of the truck screamed in horror and took off running.

My workers saw the whole thing unfold and they ran over to help me get out of the car. I had glass all over me, and my face was a mass of blood. Even my mouth was full of glass. I was able to stand up, and right away I had a feeling I was not hurt as badly as it looked. They were trying to find a Pepsi to clear the glass from my throat. Suddenly, a little white-haired man appeared, and with a smile he said, "The angels of God have protected you this night," in perfect English. Then he vanished, gone as quickly as he had come. The streets of Port au Prince were empty at that time of night and yet he could not be found.

I can assure you that there's no such thing as calling for an ambulance in Haiti, so my people took me in a taxi back to where I was staying. With great effort, I finally got the glass out of my throat enough to where I could talk. I took a hot shower, which helped to wash away the 188 glass shards that were embedded in my back. Praise God, just as I had initially believed, my injuries looked much worse than they actually were.

God had indeed protected me from severe injury, or possibly even death, just as the little old "man" had said. I can only surmise that he was an angel sent from God with that blessed message that night. The Bible says that the angels encamp round about us, and that they minister to those who are heirs of salvation. Hebrews 1:14 *"Are they not all ministering spirits, sent forth to minister for them who shall be heirs of salvation?"* What great security we have in knowing this. My three workers were shaken up quite a bit and declared that they would never forget what they had seen.

Angel Protection

I have had the great privilege of working as coordinator for foreign crusades for an international Evangelist, and I have been to the African continent more than sixty times. The first time I was sent to Uganda, sometime in the early 90's, I had a great deal of difficulty due to the airlines not meeting their schedules. As a result, I arrived in Entebbe after midnight, when I should have been there at 8:30 in the evening. At that late hour, there were no taxis or buses available. There were only a handful of people on my flight, and I found myself at a nearly deserted airport with no way of getting to Kampala. I came across a man with an old rag-tag Volkswagen and he agreed to take me to Kampala. I was to spend six weeks in Uganda and so I had several suitcases full of food and other supplies. Unfortunately, these suitcases were very visible through the windows of the car.

We started toward Kampala, and there were no streetlights at all along this lonely stretch of road. For many miles, we were the only car to be seen. About halfway to our destination, I spotted a car advancing very quickly from behind. The car passed us and suddenly blocked our way, forcing us to stop. Out of the car jumped three men with pistols, intent no doubt on robbing us. On instinct, I shouted at the driver to move backward. Petrified with fear, he immediately obeyed. As our car went in reverse, the headlights shined right in the faces of these men and they were now fully exposed.

As we backed up, I looked to my left and I saw a man who appeared to be a soldier. He was in uniform and carried a rifle on his right shoulder. He was not looking at me or even toward the road. Instead his gaze was off to the left. As soon as I saw him, I instructed the driver to stop. I have no idea what the would-be robbers may have seen or heard, but suddenly they jumped in their car and took off. Greatly relieved, I looked back to my left, and there was no soldier there. In fact, there was *nothing* there because we were out in the middle of nowhere. Again I feel with great certainty that the Lord sent one of His protecting angels to watch out for me as I was on a divine mission for Him.

CHAPTER 8

NO END OF MIRACLES

---·❦❧·---

"For the eyes of the Lord run to and fro throughout the whole earth, to shew himself strong in the behalf of them whose heart is perfect toward him."
II Chronicles 16:9

When one is called of God, part of that calling is to walk by faith and to trust the Lord to provide all things needed. You must learn to go from faith to faith, and then just keep going that way.

For much of our lives in ministry, Mary and I have been without things we may have wanted, but we can say with complete honesty that God has always provided the things we really needed. We never asked for a dime from the churches we pastored, and three years out of a particular ten year period, we didn't have a salary of any kind. We trusted God and lived by faith, and He always saw us through.

As humans, we tend to dread and even loathe times of want and adversity, but as children of God, we really shouldn't, for it is during these times that the Lord does His best work for us.

God Is Mindful Of All Our Needs

At a particularly lean time in our lives, and we were really living on a shoestring. Mary was having problems with her teeth and finally had to go see a dentist. It was discovered that she had eight cavities, and it was going to cost $300 to correct her problems. At that time, $300 was a lot of money, and we simply did not have it.

During service one evening, Mary came forward for prayer. I asked her what she needed, and she said, "My teeth." Everyone gathered around and we prayed for a miracle. As the presence of God came upon her, she felt His power and she said later it felt like someone was in there working on her teeth. We looked in her mouth and all eight cavities were gone! God had moved with re-creative power and given Mary eight new teeth. We were so surprised because we had never heard of anything like that. We'd heard of people getting fillings, but God had gone far beyond even that.

Rain That Softened A Hard Heart

Mary's parents were Elmer and Verlie Smith. After Mary and I got saved, our hearts desire was to see her parents come to the Lord. The only time either of them was in church was for special occasions. I had a particular burden for my father-in-law, Elmer. I had such a strong desire to witness to him, but whenever I would bring up the topic of our conversion, he would just laugh and say that when he died, it would be like when an animal dies. He had absolutely no belief in the afterlife.

Mary carried a heavy burden for her daddy for she loved him so much. One time I told him how I was able to stop taking all the medication the Marines had given me the night I got saved. I had thrown it all away because I didn't need it anymore. He just laughed and chalked it off to my imagination. Then we told him about Mary's miracle for her teeth. He seemed to take that a little more seriously, but was still unconvinced. He and his wife were wonderful, moral people who helped their neighbors and were honest in business, but they were not saved.

On one occasion, we came to their house to stay for the weekend. In Kansas that year, they had the driest year ever. Everything was literally burnt up and there were deep cracks in the earth. Mary's father lost his entire corn crop. There hadn't been any rain for months. As I once again brought up the subject of salvation, my father-in-law put a challenge to me: He said, "If you make it rain tonight, I'll believe." I was surprised to hear this and I asked him, "You really will believe if we pray and it rains?" and he said, "Yes." With this affirmation, Mary and I went outside and knelt in the yard and joined hands together with burdened hearts.

With all that was within us, we wanted it to rain. No end to the drought was in sight and there had been no forecast of rain whatsoever. Nonetheless, we began to pray in earnest, and in about 10 seconds, a cool breeze swept across our face. We looked up to see that a cloud had formed, and as sure as God is on His throne, it began to sprinkle before we could get out of the yard. We went inside quietly rejoicing! There was no need to say anything. It had begun to rain and it rained all the night through. In fact, it was what they called a "soaker" for two solid days.

At breakfast the next morning, we had plenty of ham, eggs, and biscuits, but not very much conversation. We didn't say anything—it wasn't necessary. We only saw the family periodically after that, but in 1959, on his deathbed, I had the opportunity to pray with my father-in-law, and we do feel that he received Jesus and made it safely home to heaven.

You cannot bargain with God

In one place where I was wanting to build a church an elderly lady called one morning and said she wanted to see us. We went to her home, and before entering into discussion, she said she wanted to show us her back. She uncovered herself, and it was truly the most horrendous sight I had ever seen. Her flesh appeared to be rotting and was covered with some sort of tar-like substance, presumably a remedy to try and bring healing. She told us she had cancer and wanted God to heal her. I assured her that the Lord could do just that.

She then told me she had a piece of ground that would suit my needs for the church, and that she wanted to donate the ground to us. Naturally that sounded wonderful, but for some reason, I questioned her motive for wanting to give the land as a gift. This question kept persisting in my mind, so I decided to ask her about it. Her response was that she felt like it would help her gain entrance into heaven, that it would give her favor with the Lord. Upon hearing this, I told her that I could not accept the gift on those terms. She became very angry and threw quite a fit right there in our presence. Clearly she did not grasp the concept of grace, God's unmerited favor through His Son, Jesus Christ.

Shortly after this we acquired the land we needed, a piece of ground that God willed for us to have. Two or three Sundays went by after our meeting, and then this lady showed up in service. I was truly happy to see her. At the end of the service, she came forward and I asked her what she needed. Her reply was that she wanted to be saved. Sometime during those days she had come to realize that salvation comes through faith and not through works. She surrendered her heart to the Lord that day, and shortly after that, the Lord saw fit to take her home to be with Him.

A Dry-Land Passage

I have never talked about this next miracle very much because I don't know how to fully express something that was so fantastic and so unbelievable. But I assure you as God is my witness, it is a true story. One Sunday night, Mary and I gave someone a ride home from church. Our ten year old son, Glen, was in the car as well. It was a rainy night and we were in a rural area. I knew a shortcut back to our place, so after we dropped the person off, I headed in that direction. The shortcut was down a dirt road, and unfortunately, I only got about a block down the road and then the car sunk in the mud up to the axles. We were hopelessly stuck and I could see that the car wasn't going anywhere. Our one option it seemed was to go the rest of the journey on foot. We were at least a mile-and-a-half from home, and most of our walking would be on that muddy road.

We were not at all prepared for this situation. We didn't have so much as an umbrella with us. None of us could have dreamed of what was about to happen. We didn't even ask for this miracle, but God was so very mindful of us. I told my family, "Rain or no rain, we're going to have to walk home."

I got out of the car first, and I noticed right away that no water was hitting me. Next Mary and Glen got out and they experienced the same thing. I looked and it was raining all around us, but within about an eight or ten-foot circumference around us, there was no rain falling. We started walking and this dry patch stayed with us. We kept going for many blocks, and all the way to our home, God had His great umbrella over us. I had never witnessed a miracle like this, nor could I think of anything I'd ever heard about that could compare. When we got to our porch, our clothes were still completely dry!

I found this miracle to be so profound and yet amusing at the same time. Mary and Glen had the good sense to climb up on the porch and get under the overhang. I stayed out in the open, laughing in wonderment. What a miracle! It was the most amusing thing I ever thought to witness. As I lingered on the walk, the "umbrella" suddenly came down and I was soaked to the bone just like that. I knew then that surely the Lord must have a sense of humor.

A Promise That Held On For Us!

During times of leanness, it was always exciting to see how God would provide for our needs. When we built the church in Valley Falls, we took no salary for ourselves, and any money that came our way had to go to cover utilities and so forth. We didn't tell people about our needs or about the things we didn't have. We trusted in the Lord and made a daily practice of holding on to His promises of provision.

One Saturday, I asked Mary and Glen to go and visit Brother and Sister Grimm. Mary was just learning to drive at that time, and since it was about seventeen miles to their place out in the country, I thought that would give her a good opportunity to practice driving our stick-shift. In the meantime, I was going to walk around town and invite people to church. I stood and watched Mary drive off, and I must say, it was quite comical to see the car jerking back and forth as she practiced her skills with a clutch.

Later in the day, I arrived back home just ahead of Mary and Glen. As she pulled in the drive, I looked at the rear bumper and there clung a chicken to the back of the car! She appeared to be holding on for dear life. Mouth-watering as it was, we knew we couldn't eat it because it belonged to the Grimms. The next day was Sunday, so we made plans to return the feathered stowaway to its rightful owners.

As the Grimms pulled into the church the next morning, they started apologizing and said they had intended to give us a fryer chicken the day before but had forgotten. I told them not to worry—it came!

Even in "Sin City" God Can Supply

God's ways are certainly not our ways, and you just never know how He might move to supply the needs of His children. Often He works in ways that we would never expect. I know of a couple who were in ministry and did much traveling by car in their work for the Lord. During one of their journeys, their car was in desperate need of new tires, but they did not have the more than $350 it was going to cost to replace them.

As they were driving through Nevada late one night, they came to Las Vegas and decided to stop and stretch their legs a bit and perhaps take some small refreshment. In the lobby of the place where they'd stopped was a slot machine, and just on a whim, the husband dropped in a coin to show his wife how it worked. When he pulled the arm in demonstration, all the bells and whistles went off for he had hit the jackpot! And it's no surprise that the payout was just the amount they needed for those new tires. Mary and I know this couple very well.

More Blessed To Give Than To Receive

There are times when God uses us as the channel through whom He will flow His promised provision to someone else, and one such instance occurred with us. Our daughter Cheryl was the last to marry and leave home, and then our nest was empty again. We were down to just one more mortgage payment and we would own the house we were living in. As I'm sure most people could understand, it was a good feeling to be in such a position, and I left for crusades in Haiti with a sense of calm assurance.

While in Haiti, I laid on my bed one evening and asked the Lord to speak to me differently that night than He had ever spoken before. I remember asking Him not to tell me what I want to hear, but what I need to hear. After making this request, the Lord spoke audibly and told me to give my house to a certain couple who were very sick and who were going through a difficult time. This came as a mild shock, I must say, for we had never been asked to do something like that before. In my mind's eye, it was as though I could see the Lord smiling at the expression on my face. I was completely willing to obey God's instructions, but I said, "Lord, you will have to tell Mary."

I did not share this experience with anyone, and I returned home a few days after that. I told Mary that God had spoken to me while I was away, and her immediate response was, "I know." Needless to say, this was a pleasant surprise. I decided to have Mary tell me what God had said to her. She said, "We are to give our home to..." and she named the couple. It was truly amazing that a husband and wife so many miles apart could hear from heaven at the same time, but that is how it should be for the Lord says that "Two now shall be made one."

Armed with the knowledge of what God wanted, we were eager to get it done. Having complete certainty that this was all directed of the Lord, it was not something difficult to do. Rather, it was a joy and an honor to help these dear people. We made all the necessary arrangements concerning the house and took the paperwork to the couple. You can imagine how shocked they were. At first they were very hesitant, insisting that they could not take our home from us, but we assured them that God had instructed us to do this. In addition to the home itself, we left all the "extras" in it for them to enjoy. With great happiness and assurance that God would supply our needs, Mary and I started over again.

Finding a Needle in a Indian Haystack

God's promises of provision stretch far beyond the material things and needs for the body. Sometimes we need wisdom, guidance, direction or favor, all of which the Lord has promised to supply as we place our trust in Him. It could be an item we've lost or a person we're trying to locate and we have no idea which way to turn. Such was the case with me one time in South India.

I was preaching in Kerala State in 1966 and was joined by Rev. Gordon Lindsay. We preached together for a period of time, and then he had to go on to London. Before leaving, he told me he urgently need to reach someone in Columbo, Sri Lanka and he asked if I could possibly go there and try to locate a Rev. Williams. The matter had to do with the translation of religious material and the printing of 20,000 pieces of literature, and he only had the name Rev. Williams, but he understood that he was known in Christian circles. I agreed to the task of trying to locate this brother.

I flew into Columbo, or more accurately, into the airport which is about twenty-two miles from the city. After my arrival, I sat there wondering how I was going to find this Rev. Williams in a city of two million. Just then, a young American man came off a charter plane, and for some reason, I felt the urge to talk to him. I introduced myself and told him why I had come to Columbo. He did not know Rev. Williams himself, but he told me that he was representing a ship that was docked in Columbo, and he suggested I travel there with him. There were about 150 people on the ship from different nations, and his idea was to have me ask these folks if any of them knew the man I was looking for.

We got to the ship and I went aboard and made my announcement. Remarkably, a man stepped forward to say that he had just left a Rev. Williams at a hotel about a block away. I took off running up the street and I found Rev. Williams — *the* Rev. Williams! — and I was able to take care of all the necessary business Rev. Lindsay had charged me with. God had provided just the young man I needed at just the time I needed him to make this meeting possible. He tells us in

Proverbs 3:6, "Acknowledge him in all thy ways and he will direct thy paths," and this was one time that this undeniably took place.

CHAPTER 9

A SMALL NATION
IN GREAT NEED

---

*"Inasmuch as ye have done it unto one of the least of these
my brethren, ye have done it unto me."*
Matthew 25:40

More than fifty years ago, I was reading about Haiti in the newspaper. At that time, there was an embargo against the island nation, and everything we were reading was negative. Francois Duvalier, also known as Papa Doc, was a self-proclaimed "president for life," or a dictator, as we would say. It was very clear that the people of this tiny country needed help in a big way.

One day, I was introduced to Haiti's ambassador to the United States, Mr. Arthur Bonhome from Washington D.C. I was told that he had become a born-again Christian, and that he was willing to come and lecture about the situation in Haiti upon request. We connected very well, and subsequently, We flew him into Topeka. We organized civic and religious leaders for a gathering, from the governor's office on down.

We had a huge turnout to hear him talk about Haiti, but we were not un-opposed: Ninety illegal Haitians from New

York flew in to oppose this meeting. At this time, messages out of New York were being sent to Haiti calling for Papa Doc's assassination, and bombs were being dropped around the national palace. Mr. Bonhome gave a wonderful speech, and surprisingly, the opposition held their peace while he gave his talk. He came to my church and gave his personal testimony of how he came to Christ.

Mr. Bonhome invited me to his hotel suite on the morning of his departure, and when I arrived, he handed the telephone to me. Imagine my shock when I realized that on the other end of the line was the dictator of Haiti. The ambassador called the President every morning. Feeling rather speechless for the moment, I didn't really know what to ask this man. Trying to think quickly, I managed to ask him if there was freedom of religion in Haiti. His reply was, "You must come and see."

Mr. Arthur Bonhomme, Haitian Ambassador to Washington D.C. and Reverend Max L. Manning disembarking from the plane in Topeka Kansas

After we hung up the phone, Mr. Bonhome said that the President wanted me to come the very next day and be a guest at the national palace. Papa Doc gave authorization for my ticket and the necessary arrangements. I quickly telephoned my best friend Reverend Darrell Friend to join me on this mission, and shortly thereafter we found ourselves on the way to Port au Prince, Haiti.

It was immediately evident that Haiti was a country governed by great fear. It was military rule at the time, and on the streets were the Tonton Macoute to help keep the "order." We were whisked off the airplane to a limousine, completely bypassing normal customs procedures, and taken directly to the presidential palace. We were getting the treatment of an international dignitary, so I really began to think that they had made a mistake about my identity.

Shortly after our arrival, We were in a private audience with Papa Doc, the most feared man in the world at that time. Apologetically I said, "Mr. President, perhaps there has been a misunderstanding about my position in life." I felt sure he must have taken me for a politician. He said, "Oh no, Arthur told me all about you, and I know you are a man of God, a pastor." That being said, I was able to relax and engage in conversation.

The president and I talked for about two hours. I had not prepared anything ahead of time, so the Lord gave me what He wanted discussed. I talked about the powers that be, how God lifts up people and how he puts down people. I explained that he had been permitted by God to be president. He was formerly a medical doctor and a voodoo priest, and I explained that God had placed him in power and that he was responsible for the well-being of the people. It's almost beyond belief, but I was most definitely preaching to him.

Papa Doc was very cordial and open-hearted to the things I shared, and at the conclusion, he said, "I want you to help my people." At that moment in time, I had absolutely no idea how I could be of help to his people. I had just returned from a mission trip to old Mexico, and I had no money whatsoever. But if one has a willing heart, God will take care of the rest. The president offered me land and other things with which to start a work, so I assured him that I would get involved in some way.

At the end of our session, I asked him if I could pray over him, and he nodded in acceptance. By this time, he had made his way from where we'd been talking over toward his desk. I reached for his hand, and as I did so, loud alarms began to sound. Then the four doors to the office opened and men with rifles burst through. He motioned the soldiers back. I prayed with Papa Doc then, and I really prayed in the Spirit with God's anointing upon me in a marvelous way. I prayed that the Lord would reveal Himself to him, that he would open his eyes to the saving grace of Jesus Christ, and that he would be able to lead his people in the right way. When I concluded the prayer, I opened my eyes to see that there were tears over the dictator's face.

Remarkably, Papa Doc was a friend of mine all the remaining days of his life. After his passing, his son, Jean Claude "Baby Doc", took over, and we maintained a friendly relationship as well.

That was the great open door into Haiti, a door only God could have set before me. That same trip, We went to the ghetto area and had a great revival. We had a wonderful crowd of about 2,000, and we were able to feed the people and give them Bibles.

The Witness Of The Spirit

Many years ago, I was crusading in the interior rural areas of Haiti. This was far out in the jungle in areas where people did not speak English. I preached and encouraged the people to receive the gift of the Holy Ghost. I explained that tongues were the initial evidence, and they would have greater power in their lives to honor and serve God. The people were very eager to receive. It was a group of about 200 standing out in the open, and they began to yield to the Holy Spirit and were being baptized. It was marvelous to behold!

I walked among the people and I came across three individuals who were speaking in English, very fluent English. This was so shocking. I had heard tell of foreigners who had spoken in English when receiving the Holy Ghost, and I was getting to witness this for myself. It was truly exciting. These people were exalting the Lord Jesus Christ, glorifying Him on high. It was all about Jesus. For me it was confirmation that when we speak in another tongue, we are indeed speaking unto God. Afterward, I went to each of them and not one of them could speak a word in English. It was a blessed experience to say the least.

Known By Name

In 1967, I took a team of young men to the southwestern part of Haiti to a place called St. Louis to plant a church. I asked the Lord where He wanted the, and He moved on me to stop at a certain point across from a cemetery. My workers and I were walking along the area, which was near the beach, and I was going to leave the young men there to start spading and so forth in preparation for the work to come.

In Haiti, the majority of people speak Kreole or French. Not many speak English, but out in an area like this, no one does. As I was giving my workers directions, suddenly an old man ran toward us, looking very hateful. The man said, "Max Manning, go home! We don't want you here!" I began to feel very unappreciated, but then it dawned on me that this man could not possibly speak English. He hollered out his instructions to me again. I whirled around and cried, "You foul unclean spirits, come out of him!" He fell under the power as though he'd been knocked out, and I told the young men to lead him to the Lord as soon as he came to. He gave his heart to Jesus, received the Holy Ghost right then and there, and went on to become a preacher!

I tried to speak to the man later, and just as I had suspected, he could not speak a word of English. He became a great worker for God, and established a total of six churches. So often those who are all-out for the devil turn around and go all-out for God.

This incident reminds me of how the apostle Paul cast a fortune-telling devil out of a young lady in the 16th chapter of Acts. If you think the devil doesn't know your name, you are definitely mistaken. I did not allow fear or discouragement to take hold of me that day, and as a result, a church stands in St. Louie that seats 300 and is full every Sunday. Other churches have been spawned from that one as well.

Abide In Your Calling

God has given me many abilities with which to do His work, but I am the first to admit that I am not particularly gifted when it comes to other languages. One time in Port-au-Prince, I was to speak at a large church, so I tried my very best to get a little message together in Creole. I really purposed to do this because it's always such a blessing when you can say something to the people in their language.

Sunday morning arrived, and my theme was meant to be the greatness of God, but as I began to speak and the interpretation came forth, what I had actually declared was, "Your women have big hips!" If memory serves me correctly, that's the last message I attempted in another language.

A Record-Breaker In Our Backyard

Yes, when dealing with another culture and a different language, you must allow a lot of latitude for misunderstanding and miscommunication. In 1971, I had a lovely three-acre plot in Carrefour, Haiti. The compound was made up of an orphanage capable of accommodating 120 children, an elementary school that had 300 in attendance every day, a medical clinic and a caretaker's house. That was a lot of humanity on those three acres, and it became necessary to add another sanitation out-building to the compound because we just had so many people coming and "going."

I was approached by three men who engineered and built outside toilets, and we made an agreement that this small facility would have three seats and that the drop from the seat to the area below should be 8 feet. I was going back to the United States for two weeks, and during my absence, they were to complete the job.

When I returned, I was in total shock because I saw huge mounds of dirt all around the new outhouse. I inspected the building and the hole that was dug, and I thought, "My! This is the deepest toilet I've ever seen!" I couldn't comprehend how this could have happened, so I called the men together and questioned them about it. The explanation was very simple actually: They thought I had said 80 feet! They assured me that I was not charged any more for the extra deepness, but my concern was what I was going to do with all that extra dirt!

We did not fill the dirt back in, and although it has not been confirmed with the folks from the Guinness Book, so as far as I know, we are still the record-holders of the world's deepest toilet.

The Power Of The Blood

In yet another project in Carrefour, Haiti, we obtained a two-acre plot where we intended to have a dental clinic, a medical clinic, a guesthouse, a school, an orphanage and a church.

We moved about 100 orphans into one of the existing buildings, but before occupying it, we had forgotten to pray over it. In our haste, we had failed to anoint the building and to plead the blood of Jesus and take authority over it through prayer. The children all went to bed that night, and about 4 o'clock in the morning, one of the young girls, about 12 years of age, began to scream in terror. Her bloodcurdling screams could be heard throughout the entire compound.

When we got to her bedside, she described having seen an old lady right over her bed that had terrified her. In spite of her young age, I thought she was going to have a heart attack she was so petrified. We prayed with her for her deliverance from fear, as well as commanding every foul spirit to leave that place. We condemned all the works of the evil one, and we never had an incident of that nature after that.

Some time later, while teaching the children about agriculture, we unearthed the bones of a large human being. Through some investigating we learned that they were the remains of a powerful witch from Jamaica who had died about a year-and-a-half earlier. She had ruled that place through witchcraft and had died without accepting Jesus Christ as her Savior. Being shown a picture of the deceased lady, it matched exactly the description our little girl had given. That incident really showed how devil-possessed human beings may die, but the spirits that inhabit their souls do not.

Use What You Have In Your Hand–Even If It's A Pair Of Pliers!

Haiti is one of the most impoverished nations in the Western hemisphere on our planet, and in all countries of such extreme poverty, there are areas where there are no doctors whatsoever. In 1969, I was in the interior, and we held a day clinic for minor things like itching, bruising, and other small medical complaints. In places like this, they look at a white man as though he can do anything.

An old snaggle-toothed man, about 65 years of age, appeared at the clinic one day, gums swollen and abscessed, wanting a tooth extracted. I said, "Yes, I can extract your tooth," but I had him sit down and I asked him if he was sure he wanted me to take it out. He agreed despite the fact that I had no Novocain or anything of the sort. I asked him to show me exactly the tooth, so he pointed and poked in the area. In the absence of any kind of anesthetic, I had someone holding each of his knees and arms. All I had was a pair of pliers and it took me about 25 minutes to get that tooth out. The poor man went through a lot, but we finally had success.

I have had many incidents similar to this one. It can be a great challenge trying to care for the neediest people in the world on the limited resources available to you. In the United States, you would never be allowed to help somebody in that manner. But when there are no medical people available, you just have to do the best you can. A very helpful book has been written to assist non-medical persons like myself, and it is so aptly called, "Where There Are No Doctors."

Hazarding My Life For The Gospel

In all my travels to Haiti, I have never come out unscathed. I think of the Apostle Paul and all that he went through for the sake of the Gospel. He had scars acquired in sin, but he had abundant scars from being the messenger of God. The enemy hates anyone who carries the Gospel in any capacity.

In 1970, I was in a place called Korai conducting glorious services. I baptized more than 700 people in the ocean right there adjacent to the crusade. There were absolutely no facilities available in that are, so at night I was sleeping outside in a sleeping bag.

Often it seems that our greatest victories get us ready for our greatest trials. I had just ended a truly wonderful day, one of my best ever. I slipped into the sleeping bag, zipped it up and went off to sleep. It must have been about 2 o'clock in the morning, when suddenly my right arm above the elbow felt like it had been shot. Out of reflex, I reached up and slapped my arm, and in doing so, I killed a large, deadly equatorial scorpion.

Almost no one has ever survived the sting of this particular scorpion. The poison spread very quickly, and within minutes I had a horrific headache and my heart began to beat very rapidly. I was beginning to lose coherency, and I called to two Haitian brothers to help me. There was no road out of this place (I had come by boat), and we had to go through the jungle to get to a road. The brothers carried me to a place called Jeremie, where they had a plane come in to get me. By this time I was totally delirious. Someone asked if I wanted to call my wife, and I said, "Yes." When they got her on the line, all I said was, "Mary, I am sick," and hung up the phone.

I was flown back to the United States and hospitalized. They found the scorpion's stinger still buried in my arm and were able to remove it, but beyond that, there wasn't a lot they could do for me. Nothing could relieve the pain, and my arm looked as if it would rot right off my shoulder.

They released me from the hospital, but I was still just as sick as when I went in. I thought of a pastor friend of mine, so I called him. In great distress, I told him I had been stung by a scorpion. My friend got quiet and said, "Wait a moment," and then he prayed, "Jesus, this is your servant. Heal him." With that simple, brief prayer, the pain began to vanish from my head, and within three or four days, my arm was completely healed without so much as a scar.

One of my worst experiences occurred as I was traveling across the country in Haiti alone. It was raining and the waters were very high, up to the hood of the car. It was around 10 at night, and I was extremely tired. I stopped at a little grass hut, and asked the man there if I could come in. He invited me in and graciously gave me a pillow. With all the moisture in the area, the mosquitoes were terrible. They bit me the whole night through.

I would learn later that at least one of these minuscule pests was carrying the virus that causes Dengue fever. After reaching Port-au-Prince, I developed a very intense fever. It quickly rose to 104 degrees, and my workers told me I needed to go home. I went home and tried my best to fight my way through the sickness. The fever soared to 107 degrees and stayed there for many days.

The nickname for Dengue fever is "the bone-crusher." A center for tropical diseases confirmed that that was in fact what I had. They put me on penicillin, not knowing that I am allergic to it. I lost the use of my legs, couldn't eat and couldn't react mentally. It would take divine intervention to bring me out of this, and the Lord had mercy and healed me completely.

The Apostle Paul mentioned in his writings how he was striped three times. Well, for me, I was bitten three times by a brown recluse spider. Three of these spiders bit me in Chipata, Zambia, and then twice I was bitten in Haiti. Each time, I had to have divine healing in order to recover.

All of this was in the line of duty, serving God and working for him. When these various incidents occurred, I knew I was in the center of God's divine will, and Peter said to not think it strange when the fiery trials come. Paul said he was hindered in the work of God, and we certainly will be, too.

When The Law Are The Lawless

I have witnessed five overthrowings of government, Haiti's infamous coups, most of which were carried out by the military. On one occasion, I had a medical bus full of equipment, that we used as a tool of evangelism. We were able to assist the people medically, preach the Gospel to them, and we often showed the Jesus film. The bus was a great asset to my ministry.

I arrived back at my headquarters one day and discovered that armed military men had come and taken our bus at gunpoint. In a lawless atmosphere like Haiti, whoever has the gun wins. They take what they want, and that's just how it is. I was extremely upset at this news and I determined to see the general of the army.

I arrived at the general's office with adrenaline on high. We had suffered a tremendous loss and I was very upset. I passed right by five secretaries and two security men, pulled his door opened and sat down in front of him. I said, "General, I'm an American missionary and I want to talk with you." He motioned for those who were trying to stop me to go out.

I asked the general if he was above the law, to which he replied no. I told him that as a guest in his nation, I also was not above the law. I went on to inform him that he had at least two majors and their subordinates who did feel that they were above the law, and I proceeded to tell him how the bus had been confiscated. I gave him the names of the two majors, as well as my phone number, and asked him what he was going to do about it. He said, "I will get back with you." I said, "When? Tomorrow? The next day?" and all he said was, "Soon."

Haiti has more corruption than any other nation I know of. The general, of course, was in collaboration with the majors. I did not hear back from him, and a year went by as I continued to search for my bus. I finally found it one day on a road leading outside the city. They had stripped it and worn it out completely. They had taken the bus between Haiti and the Dominican Republic time and again, and had literally worn it out.

The general and I had both conceded that day in his office that neither of us was above the law, but the problem was that there was no law in the land at that time. I had no choice but to commit the matter unto the Lord, leave it in His hands and hope for a better day.

Believe For Greater Things

In 1978, One of my best friends, Brother Harold Grimes invited me to travel to Northern California and Nevada. He further encouraged me and sent me to Phoenix Arizona before returning home where there was a huge convention of the Full Gospel Business Men's Fellowship International going on at that time. I went to Phoenix to a large hotel that had a huge convention hall seating possibly 10,000 people.

I checked into my room and then went to the auditorium. There were many, many men there, some of whom I recognized by photos I had seen. I went to the center section and took a seat in the midst of everyone.

The meeting convened and someone got up and began to speak. Suddenly I felt a tap on my left shoulder, and I turned around to see a lady who had pressed her way through the crowd trying to get my attention. I could see that she was a very attractive woman, and I tried to ignore her. She tapped me again and whispered in my ear, "I must talk with you. Please come to the foyer." I was very hesitant because I didn't know who might know me there and wonder why I was exiting the meeting at a hotel with a very attractive lady!

Quite reluctantly, I did go with her to the foyer. She said that her husband was a banker and he was up on the stage. She took both of my hands and said she had a word for me.

She said all she was doing was delivering a message, that God had moved on her when I walked in. She began with, "Thus saith the Lord..." and the essence of the message was that I was not open enough or believing enough for God to do greater things in my ministry. She said God wanted to do greater things, but He couldn't do them because I wasn't open and believing. God was going to bountifully bless me.

When she was finished, I was impacted by the Spirit and broken, to say the least. It was great news that God wanted to bless me in my work in Haiti. She dropped my hands and said, "That's all. God bless you," and walked away. I did not go back into the auditorium because I was so overcome and broken. I began to walk down the hallway and about halfway down was a coffee shop. I decided I would go inside and sit for a little while.

I took a seat at the counter and next to me was a very poor-looking man with rather long hair, and a beard, I believe. I didn't really look at him, and he didn't look at me, but the moment I sat down, he said, "You have not sat here by chance. I have a word from the Lord for you." He repeated everything that the lady in the foyer had said exactly, even the scripture she had quoted. He never looked at me, but he spoke very assertively, in an almost commanding tone. There were service items and coffee on the counter, but I never saw him touch any of that. He said, "That is all," and with that I was again broken in spirit and humbled before the Lord as I walked away.

To this day, I feel in my heart that this second encounter was of the "angels unaware" sort. After this experience, I couldn't even order coffee, I was so overcome. I was weeping so that I had to go to my room to gain my composure.

I left Phoenix and was flying to Miami to go onward to Haiti. During the flight, a man came and asked if he could sit next to me. I said, "Sure, if we can talk about Jesus." He said, "I am your man. I want to talk about Him." We talked about Jesus and my ministry in Haiti, about the children and the widows, and so forth. He thought it was all so wonderful, and he asked if I could use twenty tons of powdered milk, and another twenty tons of dried peaches and apples. I said, "Man, could I!" These items were of great value, and we made arrangements for him to ship them to me.

As I received this bounty for Haiti, it confirmed the two messages I had received in Phoenix. From that point on, I opened my heart for greater things from the Lord, and God gave me greater and greater vision.

Over the last more than 45 years, I have taken literally tons of provisions into Haiti, including container after container of clothing to give to the less fortunate. On one particular occasion, I took a big load of clothes out to the country to distribute. Usually we try to take all summer clothes because Haiti is tropical and thus very hot, but this day somehow some long handle underwear got mixed in. We had service that evening, and here came a young boy, about 10 years old, all dressed up for church. He had his legs through the arms of that long underwear, his arms through the legs, and out of the built-in "window" peered his little smiling face!

A Girl Named Yvrose)

Many, many years ago, I took a boat from Port-au-Prince to a place in the west called Pestel. One had to go by boat because there were no roads to this area. I was to hold a 7-day crusade and seminar where I would feed hundreds of pastors. Large numbers of people assembled for this event and we had great times in the Lord. There were no hotels in this place, and so I had to sleep in my sleeping bag.

During the day, some of the young people who had come to the crusade with their parents visited me in the place were I was resting. Among them was a young lady named Yvrose Pierre and she was about 16, as I recall. Her father was a pastor over five Haitian churches. She told me she believed God was calling her into ministry, but she needed a guitar. She wanted to teach young people to sing and play, and lead people to the Lord. I was touched by her youthful sincerity, and I more or less promised to get a nice guitar and send it to her.

Some time later, I visited a church in Canada and was talking about this young lady. I told how she was truly gifted to sing, and to play and write music, but that she could never afford to buy a guitar. To my great delight, a person in this church had a very good-quality acoustic guitar, and they wanted to donate it to this young lady so many miles from them.

Upon my return to Haiti, I sought out Yvrose and gave her the special gift. She was thrilled beyond words. She was assisting her father, and this was such an added blessing to their ministry.

Sometime of time later, I was parked at a hospital in Port-au-Prince, and a lady approached me, very thin and critically sick. I finally recognized her to be Yvrose. I prayed for her and God brought healing to her body. As we talked that day, I told her I felt she should go to a place called Jeremie to work, that the area was ripe for harvest. She decided to go there and we gave her what support we could for a period of time.

Almost immediately after she arrived in Jeremie, Everose opened a church, an orphanage and a school. As these institutions really began to flourish, we gave even more support. She had so many children to care for! In addition to the musical talents she had, she was a great preacher and was leading many people to the Lord.

One day I met a Nazarene man from Ohio named George Hawthorne and he told me that he was looking for an opportunity in Haiti. I felt that Yvrose would be just that opportunity, so I told him all about her. He had a contractor working for him, and he would be able to help with building and also with financial support. George gladly took over the responsibilities of supporting the work in Jeremie.

Time has a way of getting away from us, and twenty years went by very quickly without my seeing Yvrose in person. I did get reports about her work and how God was blessing, and then one day, she requested that I come and see the work for myself. I took several preachers with me, and we were going to have different services at the same time while we were there. Going over land takes about 22 hours, so we decided to fly in a small airplane.

Yvrose met us at the airport and it was wonderful to see her face after 20 years. She has probably the most sincere, sober face that you will find in Haiti. In fact, she rarely smiles. She had brought a truckload of people to greet us, and she also had a Jeep and another car as well. I asked her who the vehicles belonged to. She replied that they were hers. "Jesus gave them to me." That was astounding in a land of such poverty. I would soon find out that that was only the beginning of what Jesus had given to Yvrose.

We drove about seven miles into town, and when we arrived, we pulled up to a two-story building, long, wide and deep. I asked her if this was where she lived. She said, "Yes," and that she had our rooms all prepared. Then I asked her whose house it was. She said it was hers. "Jesus gave it to me." As I went inside, I was suddenly surrounded by about 70 teenage girls. I learned that they were some of her orphans, and that the boys were in another building.

We then left for service and began walking down the road. We came to a building that had about a thousand people seated inside. Before we went in, I asked her whose church it was and who the pastor was. She told me it was hers and that she was the pastor. "Jesus gave it to me." It was dumbfounding to witness all that Jesus had done for Yvrose in the last twenty years.

After the service started and she had given due reverence to her associate pastors, she began to tell all about me and how I had prayed over her and commissioned her for God to use her for His work. She humbly stated, "I owe everything to Brother Manning. He gave me my start." After her speech, she whistled and out of the crowd came about thirty young ladies, very beautiful and all dressed alike, and they picked up various musical instruments. She stepped up as the conductress, and started a song. It was the National Anthem of the United States. I jumped to my feet, along with all the rest of the Americans. After the anthem, she led them in familiar Gospel songs. The music was flawless, very disciplined, and we had a glorious time that evening.

After the service that night, we returned to her house, and she again began to tell my group how she got her start. She pulled out the guitar I had given her 20 years earlier. It was thrilling to see that small reminder of where the Lord had brought her from.

The next day, we went downtown together, and I was amazed to see how the people reacted to her presence. They almost bowed to her, and everyone addressed her as Madamme Yvrose, as though she owned the town. The whole city, in fact, called her the first lady of Jeremie, and she had reached that honored title through all that she had done for others.

It came time to return to Port-au-Prince, and when we got near the airport, I told Yvrose that I wanted to go aside and talk. I pointed out some beautiful property across the road, a whole hillside of lovely land. I asked her, "Wouldn't that be a good place to start a home or something?" She meekly informed me that that land was hers, that Jesus had given it to her years ago, and she had plans already on how to use it.

I count it an honor to be the vessel God used to help start Yvrose on her journey, and it was so wonderful to have the opportunity to see some of the fruits of our labor.

CHAPTER 10

HELPING TO PLACE
THE DISPLACED

---·⟨⟨✧⟩⟩·---

*"My little children, let us not love in word, neither in
tongue; but in deed and in truth."*
I John 3:18

General Bao Ding and his family

*A*fter a war effort that had not gone as anticipated,
our military pulled up stakes and prepared to leave
Vietnam in 1975. It became common knowledge that the
Americans were abandoning the country, and the enemies in

the north began moving southward. It became gravely necessary for hundreds of thousands of Vietnamese who had worked loyally with the Americans to flee their homeland. Had they stayed, they would have undoubtedly suffered many cruelties at the hands of the northern Vietnamese. Those who had collaborated with the United States most certainly would not have gone unpunished. Our nation tried to get as many of these people out of Vietnam as we could. There was only a brief window of opportunity for their escape, and people were hastily loaded onto planes and ships by the hundreds. Most escaped only with their lives, and if they were fortunate, perhaps a bag of clothing and other small items.

Suddenly thrust into refugee status, these displaced individuals were initially brought to Fort Chaffee, Arkansas, to the barracks of a deserted Army base. When the totals were counted, there were about a quarter-of-a-million people, men and women, and also children, many of whom were now without their parents. In their desperation, mothers and fathers had pushed their kids onto vessels ahead of themselves to insure their safe departure, not knowing if they would ever be able to find them in the faraway land they were headed for.

One evening, then-president Gerald Ford made an appeal on television for people to take the Vietnamese out of the refugee camps and into their homes in the Resettlement Program. Eager to be of assistance, Mary and I and our daughter Cheryl drove to Fort Chaffee at once.

Upon arriving at the Army base, I presented myself at the counter and said that I had come by special request. I asked them to please issue me the necessary clearance so we could go into the camp. They gave me a special badge that was actually only supposed to be for officials of their own team. The badge provided me immediate and repeated entrance into the camp.

Our Daughter Cheryl

All the refugees were anxious to be taken to homes outside the camp, and many, many people began appealing to us to please choose them. Each and every person pulled at our heartstrings, but we were only able to take one family at a time. That afternoon as we walked around the camp, we met a family of twelve named Do (pronounced Doe), and we decided that they would be our first family.

The media camped out at our house to cover the story, which generated much response from the community and the churches. Right away people started calling and asking how they could get involved, so I began to appear on radio and television to explain the process and to encourage people to take part. Without really planning it, I had become a spokesman of sorts for the Resettlement Program. I spoke in various churches as well, and just from that effort alone, at least 150 people that I know of were sponsored.

Worlds Apart

When we first started this endeavor, it was rather challenging because we knew nothing about the culture of the Vietnamese, and we really were not told anything to help get us ready to bring them into our home. I remember in preparing for their arrival, I ordered several extra beds. Mary and I gave up our bed, and Cheryl gave up hers in order to accommodate everyone. The next morning when I went to rouse them, each and every one of them was sleeping on a blanket on the hardwood floor! Of course I learned that that was how they were accustomed to sleeping.

Another big difference was in their culinary preferences. I went out and bought typical American breakfast food, and we prepared bacon, along with biscuits and gravy the first morning. When they sat down at the table, they looked suspiciously at the gravy, so I demonstrated how to eat it with the biscuits, and with a hearty □mm! assured them that it was very good. The adults smiled out of politeness, but the truth be told, they really never got into our food. We heard that there was an Oriental food store in Kansas City, so we loaded up two or three vehicles and took them there. They were so delighted and bought all kinds of things that they were used to. By the time they were done cooking, our home had been transformed into a spice house!

One time, apparently having forgotten my "women with big hips" fiasco in Haiti, I decided to exercise my linguistic skills with the Vietnamese. With great self-assurance I said, "chinckala boontock," to which everyone roared with laughter. When I questioned them about it, they said, "You speak like the mountain people in Vietnam," which was the equivalent of calling me a hillbilly.

The Vietnamese dearly loved us for being their sponsors, and the feelings were certainly mutual. We never had one problem with these wonderful people during our whole time of sponsorship. We were able to assist many delightful people, among them a dear old man who was a professor, and another time, the television anchor-woman from Saigon, Mrs. Twe, with her husband and their two teenage boys. Family after family passed through our doors. Many times the "families" that would come to stay with us were not necessarily related biologically. They may have been friends or only known each other, but there was a connection of some kind, and they called themselves families.

If memory serves me correctly, there were about thirteen resettlement areas in all throughout the country, and I certainly feel that these new members of society were a credit to our nation. They loved our people and were very responsible, hard-working individuals.

One of our programs was to help the Vietnamese children receive tutoring in the English language. Those who were blessed to be with their parents showed much devotion and respect for them, and their parents stressed the need to apply themselves in education. This many of them demonstrated by mastering the English language in only three month's time.

Our task as far as the adults were concerned was to help them find jobs. Many of these people were skilled professionals, pilots, doctors, registered nurses, and so forth, but most were without their credentials. The majority had gotten out of Vietnam with only the clothes on their back. I exhorted them to be patient and explained that they would in all likelihood have to take something of a lesser skill until they could either provide necessary credentials or pass tests for their particular expertise.

The community opened their hearts and their doors, and everyone we sponsored was able to find a job of some kind, some in hotels, others in restaurants, drugstores, and the like, and they began to prosper immediately. In a relatively short period of time, many were in their own homes or apartments, driving their own cars.

Coming from a tropical climate, most really desired to live in warmer parts of the country because the winters were so harsh in Kansas. They thrived so that many of them were able to migrate to places like New Orleans and San Diego as time went on.

The Greatest Gift We Could Give Them

Most of the Vietnamese were either Buddhist or Catholic, but we did our best to share the Gospel of Jesus Christ with them, and we did win some for the Lord. We were pastoring a church at the time, and as much as we could, we would try to have the service interpreted so they could understand.

Among those I was able to lead to Christ was a lady named Mrs. Tran. Previously a Buddhist, she received a real born-again experience and was made a new creature in Christ Jesus. While she did speak English, for some reason she was not able to pronounce Jesus quite correctly, and it always came out "Joo-joo." Regardless of how she said His name, I can assure you that she really loved her Joo-joo.

One day I got a call that Mrs. Tran had broken her leg. It was a bad break and they had put a heavy cast on it. When I got to her, I told her that Jesus is alive and that He wanted to heal her leg. I explained that His power would come down, go into that leg and she would be healed. I stressed that all she had to do was believe on Jesus just like she did when she got saved. This woman who not that long before would have been considered a heathen had such child-like faith, and without any question, she believed everything I told her. I prayed for her, the cast that she had only had on for two days came off and she was completely healed.

The largest Methodist church in Topeka had been wanting us to come and speak to them because they were giving consideration to involving themselves in the sponsorship program. In light of the great miracle she had received, I decided to send Mrs. Tran and assured them that she would really touch their hearts. I was not going to be present in the service, but I wanted to make sure that everything went well, so I sent a spy of sorts. Mrs. Tran had a smile and a personality that could capture anyone's heart, and when she stepped up and began to testify, the congregation accepted her wholeheartedly. She told how Joo-joo had come into her leg when Brother Manning prayed and that He had healed her. I thought it was really something how God was able to get into the hearts of those Methodist brethren through a small, little lady who had come from half-a-world away.

All in all, it was just a beautiful experience to be a part of the Vietnamese resettlement. From what we were told, Mary and I were the first U.S. citizens to take Vietnamese out of the refugee camp, and when it was all said and done, we had sponsored a total of 100 individuals and helped them to carve out a new life in their new country.

CHAPTER 11

VISIONS AND REVELATIONS

——⚜——

"For I am the Lord: I will speak, and the word that I shall speak shall come to pass."
Ezekiel 12:25

Shortly after being saved and filled with the Spirit, I went into a vision as I was praying one night. I have never fully understood this vision or the reason God gave it to me, but I have kept it in my heart all these years. The vision was as clear as any physical object that you are able to see.

To start, the Lord took me back to the beginning of man, and then just like a movie film, it would change to another period of time. After seeing what God wanted to show me, it would move again. Eventually it reached the 1700's, then the 1800's, where the mode of transportation and the style of dress were very definitive. Then the vision moved up to the present time and then beyond.

The vision continued for a long time, and it was really very interesting to watch man from his beginning and on through the different ages. Much of what I saw is difficult for me to even articulate because I had never seen things like that before.

During the vision, I saw myself preaching in foreign lands, going from nation to nation, speaking to people I had never seen before. At one point, I stood on a stage before masses of people. At that time, I could not even have imagined going forth in missionary work or organizing mass miracle crusades, but God was giving me an early look at what has actually taken place in my life.

A Message of Warning

On Sunday evening May 30th 1966, I was preaching to a capacity crowd at the church I was pastoring in Topeka, Kansas. From all appearances, the service would be a wonderful bell-ringer, but I had no idea how the tide was about to suddenly change. As I finished the message, the Spirit of God moved on me to prophesy. The Lord spoke through me and said, *"In ten days, saith the Lord, destruction shall come to this city, beginning at the southwest part of the city and continuing through the city to the northeast."*

I was shocked at what I had just spoken! To be honest, this truly distressed me because a specific date had been pronounced, and I had only recently cautioned the people to beware of date-setting prophecies. I had been preaching against personal prophecy, and teaching the people that prophecy was for edification and so forth. Now I had just given a message to which there was no condition. God had said nothing to indicate that if we joined together in prayer, this destruction would not take place. Instead it was simply a declaration that destruction was coming.

For the moment, I dropped my head to the pulpit. Then once again, the power of God came upon me and I repeated the very same message. The people knew I had never behaved like this before, and they had great confidence in me. We were all left wondering what kind of destruction could be coming to our city?

On the ninth day, I spoke to Mary, "Let's get a suitcase packed and leave town." She asked where we were going, and I said we would go and visit our parents. It didn't really matter where we went, just so we got out of town. Then I shared my reasoning with Mary: *"I had prophesied destruction was coming in ten days and if that happens, we don't want to be here, and if it doesn't happen, there will be no need to return!"*

Indian tradition had always said that Topeka could never have a tornado because it sits in a basin. However, on June 8th 1966 at 6:55 PM, that tradition was blown away as two huge tornadoes joined together, one half mile wide, and swept through the city for seventeen miles. I turned on the radio and listened to WIBW. We were 120 miles south of Topeka on Highway 75 and they were announcing news of mass destruction across the city. We knew we had to return immediately because we had friends and family in the tornado's path.

Thankfully, the loss of life was not great because of the time of day when the tornado struck. Thankfully our church was spared.

Shortly it made the newspaper that I had prophesied about the tornado, and as a result, many strange people visited me, wanting to know how I could have known about it ahead of time.

Lives Saved Through God's Revelations

While in Fairmont, Minnesota one Sunday afternoon, I laid down to take a short rest in between services. Suddenly the Lord showed me a vision of my brother-in-law slipping down a roof while attempting to adjust a television antenna. I immediately cried out to the Lord in his behalf, and I learned later that he had in fact slipped and was falling down the roof, but was caught by his wrist on a nail. God had made this known to me so I could intercede for him and he was spared from serious injury or even death.

In another instance in 1956, I was in one of the churches we had established in Kansas, and as a man came through the door, the Lord showed me that he had a 45 pistol in his pocket. As it turned out, he was the town's barber, and he confessed later that it had been his intention to commit suicide. He had gone to the extent of actually putting the gun to his head, but instead of pulling the trigger, he suddenly had a thought to come to the service instead. A prayer of deliverance was offered and a sinners prayer was prayed.

A Very Special Vision of Mary

In 1968, Mary and I chartered a big bus out of Kansas City and took a total of forty-eight people, teenagers and adults, on a mission trip to old Mexico, south of Monterey. Among other notable things that happened on that trip, a five-time murderer, who had gotten off every time, came to our meeting and got saved. This news was most welcome to the townspeople who were understandably terrified of the man.

On this same trip, we met a lady who began pointing to Mary and speaking in a very excited fashion. Neither of us speak Spanish, so through an interpreter we were able to learn what she was saying: She had had a vision that day and God had showed her a lady who laid hands on her and she received the baptism of the Holy Ghost. She was pointing to Mary because she was the lady in her vision. Without hesitation, Mary laid her hands on her and this dear Mexican lady received the Holy Ghost.

The All-Knowing, All-Seeing God

I was holding a revival in Eastern, Kansas in 1956, and during the opening service, I turned around and asked the pastor where his wife was. He responded that she was home in bed and had not been feeling well for several days. Immediately the Spirit of God revealed to me that the complaining and harassing of some in the congregation who disliked her had caused her to have a nervous breakdown. The Lord called for repentance in that church and we had a marvelous revival.

In 1966 at midday, three young men approached our door asking for some small favor. Suddenly the Spirit of God moved on me and gave them this warning: "Young men, unless you re-direct your roads and do differently, you are going to be in very bad trouble today because you are going to rob the liquor store." The young men looked startled indeed. One of them seemed to have some fear of God, and I learned later that his mother was a true, Spirit-filled, Godly woman. Sadly, these young men did not heed the merciful warning call of God. About an hour later, I learned that the liquor store had indeed been robbed, and in the process, the owner, an elderly woman, had been bludgeoned to death. The three young men were apprehended and sent to prison.

When You Least Expect It

In the church we pastored in 1965 was a couple named William and Pauline Locke, both in their sixties. They did not have many of the extras in life because they were not well-off at all. The truth of the matter is that they were very poor, but they both loved the Lord, and William sat on the board. During one particular Sunday morning message, there was a lot of freedom in the Spirit, and I was talking about miracles and God's provision.

As faith began to rise, I suddenly went into a vision. I looked at Sister Locke and said, "Before I proceed with the message, I must tell you what God is showing me about you. In the vision, you are sitting in your home in the living room. You are wearing a print dress and have a large apron on your lap. Good tidings are being given to you that you have inherited a large sum of money." Sister Locke was an old-line Pentecostal, but she spoke up and said, "Oh Brother Manning, I don't have anybody with money." I told her that was quite all right, that if it was God, it didn't have to be a relative. I assured her that she was indeed going to be blessed and that she would have to look to the Lord to determine how she was going to use the money. She and her husband rejoiced, still wondering though how this was going to be.

In about ten days, Sister Locke called and asked me to come to their home. When I arrived, her husband opened the door, giggling, and his wife was sitting in the living room just as I had seen her in the vision. Her lap was filled with $100 bills. She told me it was just as I had seen. An uncle in Springfield, Missouri whom she had forgotten about had passed away. Right after the revelation was given that Sunday morning, they got a letter stating that she had been included in the will. It was thousands and thousands of dollars she had inherited. She wanted to give me her tithe right away, and if memory serves me correctly, the tenth of her good fortune was $10,000. God had blessed abundantly! When God says something, it comes to pass.

Another sudden and unexpected revelation occurred to me in 1962. I was pastoring one of the fastest growing churches in Kansas called the Glad Tidings Assembly of God of Topeka. God was moving mightily and we were running three to four hundred people in every service. One particular Sunday night in the middle of the service, the Spirit of God moved upon me and revealed that I was to resign from the church. I made the announcement right then and there before a full house and without consulting even my beloved wife. The people gasped in disbelief because everything was moving along wonderfully and there were no problems in the church. But when God speaks and says it's time to move, we must obey, and within a matter of thirty days, we were on the road again.

Nothing Can Be Hidden From The Lord

Our God is all-knowing, and through visions and revelations He can let us know things that we would otherwise be completely unaware of. In 1966, I was pastoring the Evangel Temple in Topeka, a church I had planted. I was approached by a Pastor Wilson who had a small church in his home. He wanted to know if he could bring his flock to my church and become an associate pastor. Rev. Wilson and his wife seemed to be delightful people, and after due consideration, we took in all their members and they became a part of our body.

Later the time came for me to make a trip to India, and without reservation, I turned the church over to Brother Wilson. He assured me that all would be well during my absence. I left for India with a co-worker named Daryll Friend. I had been gone about three weeks when suddenly I went into an open vision. Daryll was with me and I asked him to document the vision for me. What I was seeing was almost unbelievable to me: Although it was morning in India, it was still nighttime in Kansas. I watched my associate pastor walking up to a house with his wife, and there were thirty-eight people walking behind him. All of these people were members of my church. They all went into the basement of the home, and then the vision went away. We fully documented the vision, and I told Daryll that this man was meeting secretly to establish another church and he thought nobody knew.

When it came time for me to return home, I called my wife and I told her to have Rev. Wilson meet me in the church parking lot. When I arrived, he was there to greet me and very cordially asked how everything had gone. I told him that I needed to talk to him, and I stressed the fact that I had spoken with no one else since my arrival home. This being understood, I began to relate to him in detail the vision God had showed me. I said, "You and your wife were leading a group of thirty-eight adults." He dropped his head, obviously dumbfounded. He then admitted that he had been meeting with individuals on the side to try to restart a church. Though I was dismayed to hear this from him, I was not at all surprised because God's visions are never wrong.

I lectured him that what he had done was a form of betrayal, that he should have first talked to me. If in fact God was calling him to start another church, the proper way would have been for us to send him off with our blessings. He acknowledged his wrong and shortly thereafter set off to start his own work. Sadly, his work never prospered and came to naught after just a couple years.

On another occasion, an associate pastor I had ordained began to secretly solicit members of the church to start withholding their tithes and offerings in order to assist him in establishing an independent church. As with the other gentleman, he did not go about this in the manner the Bible instructs. As before, the Lord visited me one night and showed me what was happening. I called him into the prayer room and told him all that God had shown me. His face became red and he admitted that it was true. He confessed that his plan was to break away that very Sunday without any explanation, which would have left me with the burden of explaining their departure to the remaining members.

Despite the fact that God had uncovered his plan, he remained determined to go. I entreated him for my sake and for the sake of the church to please allow us to send them off with our blessing, but he would not yield to this suggestion. The church he started lasted only about a year and a half. Some of those who had followed him returned to our church in disillusionment, but others were simply too embarrassed to return. We must go about things the Bible way if we wish to prosper and have the favor of God.

Watch And Pray

Just a few years ago, I got a call about midnight. The frantic lady on the other end of the line said that there was a young lady in her home who was devil possessed, and that in a rage she had destroyed almost all the furniture in the home. Since both were women, I didn't want to go to the home alone, so Mary went with me. The house was within walking distance, and all the way there, I kept softly saying, "The blood."

When we approached the house, the door was closed. The lady who had called was absolutely petrified as she let us in, and across the room stood the young lady who was devil possessed. She was only about 25 years old, but she was a large, powerful woman. As I looked at her, she twisted her face and mockingly said, "The blood." There was no way she could have heard me with physical ears as I came down the walk. I threw my left hand on her head and started to say, "You foul demons..." and before I could finish, she slammed a thick glass candy dish into my forehead. It knocked me to the floor and blood was gushing everywhere. Somehow the Lord's instructions to "watch and pray" took on new meaning for me at that moment. I arose much wiser and fully alert to what was really going on. God gave me power over the many demons that were in her and they were cast out through the divine blood of Jesus.

Max's Taxi Service

Several years ago, I was in the Dominican Republic for crusades and seminars. The Dominican sits on the other two thirds of the island of Hispaniola. With me was Rev. James Akers from Missouri. When we had completed our mission, we crossed the border back into Haiti and started toward our headquarters in Port-au-Prince. We had a five or six-hour drive ahead of us because the roads were so bad in places that we could only travel about 15 miles an hour in the old Ford F100 cargo van that I had at that time.

On this day, I was wearing a pair of white trousers and a white shirt, which was rather unusual for me. This was not how I commonly dressed. As we were driving along, I looked up ahead and was surprised to see three men standing on the left side of the road. I thought it rather strange because the surrounding area was very desolate. The men began to beckon to me to slow down. At first I really didn't know whether to pull over or not, but a visual scan of the area revealed that there were no other people or vehicles around, so I elected to stop.

I pulled up beside the men, and as they looked into the van, they said, "Sir, we want to talk to you. You, the one dressed in white." They asked me to please hear their story, and then one man began to explain that one of the other two had had a vision the day before. In the vision, a man appeared and said, "Tomorrow about this time you will see a cream-colored vehicle coming from direction of Las Cahobas, and the driver will be wearing white trousers and a white shirt." The man in the vision went on to tell him that the man in white was a true man of God and would take them to Port-au-Prince for a special meeting that the three of them were to attend.

Well, there was certainly no denying that a man dressed all in white had come from the direction of Los Cahobas in a cream-colored vehicle! As I sought to verify their story, I learned that they were three Spirit-filled Pentecostal men who had been in ministry nearby and needed a ride into Port-au-Prince. Brother Ackers and I welcomed them into the van, and we enjoyed wonderful fellowship and praise for the Lord as we traveled the rest of the journey into the city.

CHAPTER 12

STORIES WITHIN THE FAMILY

Mary, Glenn and myself 1953

"Bless the Lord, O my soul, and forget not all his benefits."
Psalm 103:2

Shortly after Mary and I dedicated our lives to the Lord we learned that we would not be having biological children of our own. While we were praying Mary had a vision and the Lord ministered to her and the Lord said "You will not have biological children but you will be the mother of many children". It was not in our heart's to work through an adoption agency but we believed that God would open the door to this in His own way. Glenn was our first child, and he was about eight years old when he came to live with us. It was a bit awkward for me to become a father of an eight year old in one day, I did want to be a good father and I knew that there would have to be rules in our home that I would have to share.

"LOOK DADDY.....
THERE HE GOES !"

I explained to him from the start that there were no secrets in our household, only openness, that we believed in honesty and integrity, and I stressed to him that he must never, never tell a lie. Well, to my great disappointment, one day while still a small boy, Glenn told a lie. It was over something that was very insignificant, and he didn't need to tell that lie. I took him to the basement, and I said, "Son, you've done what I asked you never to do," and I tried to help him understand that he didn't have to lie. The two of us wept as I talked, and then I prayed over him and gave him scripture to think on. I also warned him that if there were a next time, it would be the belt he got instead of a talking-to.

I felt confident that we had gained ground, but the very next day, the same thing occurred. As before, it was just something quite insignificant, but a lie is a lie. The Bible tells us that *"ALL liars are going into the lake of fire"* (Revelation 21:8), and so I couldn't just let it go. When he was caught in this lie, as per my promise, I took him once again to the basement, and I asked him why he had lied. He replied that the devil had made him do it. Calling to mind the previous day's warning, Glenn's eyes were wide with fear. I had him bent over my knee, but his head was turned back in my direction, and he could see that I was taking off my belt.

I questioned him once more, "Son, you say the devil made you do it?" and he affirmed, "Yes, daddy." "Well," I said, "I tried to pray the devil out of you, but that didn't work. I tried to use the Word, but that didn't work either." I then told him that I had no other choice but to beat the devil out of him. This being a very serious matter, I was intent on giving him a pretty good stroke or two, but as I lifted the belt, he screamed, **"Daddy, there he goes!"**

Delivered Of Fear

When our daughter Debbie was about 25 years old, the enemy began torturing her mind with fear and torment. It progressed to a point where she was hearing voices telling her that she was going to die. "You have cancer. You are going to die." would repeat over and over again like a broken record. I told her that it was an evil spirit telling her those things, and I told her that she wasn't going to die, that she

Our Daughter Debbie in intercession in our Prayer Room - 1966

did not have cancer and not to claim any cancer. The Lord

rebuked those evil spirits and delivered her in a moment's time. She was completely free after that. She is now twice the age she was then and she was able to raise a lovely family in the fear of the Lord.

Only A Miracle Would Do

My Sister Patsy

In 1954, my sister Patsy received a fantastic miracle that really shook everyone who heard about it. Her oldest son was just a small boy at the time. Her husband Howard was serving in the United States Airforce stationed at George Air force Base in Victorville, California. Patsy became very sick. The doctors at the military hospital thought she was pregnant at that time however she was so swollen that she had to return to the doctors, they immediately admitted her and a total of seven doctors found that she had a quick growing cancer in her uterus. Today with a diagnosis like she received, they would do a complete hysterectomy. The approach to certain diseases was different in that day, and they kept her in the hospital for three months.

Patsy's condition steadily worsened and at one point her legs were so swollen that they burst open from the swelling. The doctors declared she was dying and called the family.

Mother was already there, trying to be some comfort to my sister in her dark valley of sickness. I immediately drove to California with my dad and my brother Billy. Dad and I entered Patsy's room, dad took one look at Patsy and ran out and down the hall crying. He was not prepared for what he saw. I knew my sister's condition must be very, very dire, but I entered her room with eyes of faith. I laid a hand on her head and said, "Jesus, you made Patsy's body, and I believe you can make her well and bring her to normal." Later that evening, the family went home, leaving our dear loved one in the Lord's capable hands alone with her husband.

Two hours following the prayer of faith Patsy went into a type of labor as though she were delivering a baby. The hospital staff thought she was dying, and at this point, even her husband told God that He could have her. What was actually taking place though was Patsy's body was purging itself of the cancer. She passed two washbasins full of cancerous waste. God had moved! The next morning they took her to do a D&C, and the doctors came back just shaking their heads. No one could explain what had happened, <u>but we knew</u>.

The doctors advised Patsy and her husband not to have any more children, but they prayed and shortly after that, God gave them a beautiful daughter. And then He blessed them with another son. And she was able to carry both children full-term. The Word of God tells us that He is able to do exceeding abundantly above what we can ask or even think (Ephesians 3:20), and He certainly proved this in the life of my sister Patsy.

Spared By Love Divine

My younger brother Billy had a frightening experience some years ago that you might say was his wake-up call. Billy was an excellent painter and paint contractor In 1961, at the age of twenty-four, he dedicated his life to the Lord and was filled with His Blessed Holy Spirit. But then he started a certain job and his co workers were for the most part unsaved and for a period of time they were hounding him to go out with them for a beer at the end of the day. He was in the midst of a fierce personal battle of temptation, wanting to do what was right, but being pulled in the wrong direction by these men.

But a merciful God not wanting His little sheep to go astray began to draw on him with cords of divine love.

Billy Manning at Christ's Empty Tomb in Jerusalem 1967

The Spirit of God caught him up in a vision while he was on a thirty five foot high scaffold and suddenly he felt his spirit easing out of his body. He became surrounded by pitch darkness and stifling fear. As he describes the experience, he said he looked down and he could not see his body, only his spirit. He began to scream, "God, forgive me! Save me! I'm sorry! I will change!" As he cried out, felt the Lord's presence there and was utterly condemned before Him. He knew he was on his way to hell.

As he continued screaming, "Don't let me go into that outer darkness," all of a sudden he felt something come between him and God. It was Jesus Christ and He was pleading for Billy's life. Then he began to feel himself slide back into his body. He began to wiggle his fingers to make sure it was reality.

When he came to himself, he didn't really know what had happened. He began to ask the men he was working with what had just happened to him. They told him he just dropped his brush. Billy began to dismiss the whole thing, thinking that he must have just imagined it, but as soon as that thought went through his mind, the experience began again. Again he went through a period of screaming out to God, and again he was eased back into his body. He climbed down from the scaffolding and had me called at the church office and requested that I pick him up. Billy was tall of stature and physically strong when I picked him up he was petrified with fear, I had never seen him in this state before.

Every time he tried to talk, it was the Holy Ghost flowing with a renewed flow of that heavenly language...

I took him to the church where our prayer warriors were deep in intercession for souls but immediately joined me in praying for him. Amazingly, two men who had been working with him showed up at the church at the same time, and they had no knowledge that that was where Billy had gone. They wanted prayer as well. One of them had a vision of the handwriting on the wall and he knew he was getting his last chance from God.

For a whole year, Billy had to stay with the Lord, and always had to have a Bible in his hand to have peace. God showed him some sort of timetable, but later blocked that out of his mind. When he had these out-of-body sensations, he would hear a spinning sound, like something was going around and around. Every time his mind went off of God, that feeling would overtake him. He prayed intensely, staying in tune with God, and couldn't think about the world at all.

No More Shadows In Death's Valley

Several of my loved ones have had marvelous experiences as they've left this life, and each time it makes heaven more real to me and that much sweeter. As mentioned earlier, my father died in 1977, two days before his 86th birthday. Mother and Dad had celebrated 62 years of marriage and now they were together in a care home. Daddy was partially paralyzed and bedfast from a stroke he'd had eight years before. With Mother being in the same home, she was able to attend to him and be at his bedside.

My daddy was born in an era when few had the opportunity for education. His family lived about twelve miles from the school and did not have the necessary transportation. As a result, Daddy grew up illiterate, unable to read or write. He only knew how to sign his name. Since he could not read for himself, Mother had instilled many spiritual values in him down through the years.

I was traveling to Dallas, Texas for a revival and I passed through their city to visit Mom and Dad on a Friday afternoon. his would be the last time to see dad alive in this life. His last words to me were so very special in light of the fact that he had not had the opportunity to learn to read. He said, "Heaven and earth shall pass away, but His Word will not pass away." It meant so much to my heart to hear him quoting the Bible.

The next morning at around six o'clock, Dad woke up and called my mother to his bedside. He thanked her for being such a wonderful helpmate and mother for sixty-two years. Then with full assurance, he said, "I'm going to go now." This positiveness astounded Mother and gave her a great sense of peace. Then he asked, "Can't you see them? They have come for me." Dad was seeing the angels, but Mother was not privileged to see them at that time. Dad had always been the more reserved of the two, with mother always being much more vocal regarding spiritual matters, but now he was singing and praising God aloud. He kissed my mother one last time and then set his feet on the shores of deliverance.

Another blessed experience followed shortly after dad's passing. Dad's sister, my Aunt Susie, lived to be ninety-nine years old, and her mind remained crystal-clear all her life. When her time drew near to depart this life, different family members were gathered around her. She looked around the room, and then seemed to focus in on someone. She said, "Willie, is that you?" She was referring to my dad, who had gone on before her. She looked more earnestly and said, "Oh, yes, it is you!" Then Aunt Susie began to look for Ernest their brother, who had also preceded her in death, and she finally found him. Her eyes were wide open and she was smiling so big as she reached out to her two brothers. The next moment, she was gone to be with Willie and Ernest—and Jesus—for all eternity.

I conducted Aunt Susie's funeral in the Ozarks and it was quite a gathering. I had never met all her family members previous to that time. Children, grandchildren, all the way to four generations were represented with a total of 100 individuals. Her experience as she passed away was such a testimony, and I was able to share this with her extended family and all in attendance. It is a joy to think about the glories of heaven that await those of us who know Christ.

My Brother Gene Manning

Another unique incident occurred with my brother Gene. While I was away in Swaziland, Africa my sister Wilma had suddenly passed away, and I was so hurt that I could not be there at the memorial service. When I got back home, I knew Gene was ailing, so I drove to see him in the care home where he lived. He was so frail and still grieving over Wilma's passing. After we embraced, he looked me in the eye and said, "Max, I'm going to die." I encouraged him not to talk about death, that he was going to be all right. He said, "No, God has shown me that I am going to die." Realizing his sincerity, I asked him if he was ready, and he affirmed that he was. We spent a wonderful day together that was truly blessed of the Lord. As soon as I returned to my home, I got a call from his family advising me that Gene had been taken to the hospital in Wichita. I joined the rest of his family at his bedside. We all sang a song he dearly loved, "I'll Fly Away," and assured him that it was okay to go. Quietly he slipped away and our voices were replaced with voices of the heavenly choir.

My nephew, Jerry Allen Manning, the son of my brother Gearl and his wife Etta Mae, experienced a similar home-going. He was born in 1939, and had had an illness for most of his young life. He was one of the godliest young men that we have ever known. He was Spirit-filled from his youth and had extremely high standards and high convictions, even to the point that he would wear only long-sleeved shirts. He had never gone out into sin, and the call of God was on his life as it was on his father's. One time I had him come for a week of speaking engagements in Kansas, and he was a great blessing to the youth.

Jerry's physical condition worsened until he was bedfast in a hospital in Albuquerque, New Mexico, where the family lived. My brother and his wife finally came to the place where they released him into the Lord's care, and the very next day, while sitting up in his hospital bed, he lifted his arms and began to sing, "Lord, I'm Coming Home." Line after line he sang and before he could finish the song, the Lord turned it into living reality for him.

Jerry Allen Manning

If I have learned anything to pass along to you from the past 63 years of serving the Lord in full time ministry it is this: I have learned that you cannot <u>outgive God</u>, You cannot <u>outlove God</u>, you cannot <u>overserve</u> our precious Lord. If you are in the ministry the greatest three gifts that you can aquire from the Holy Spirit to pour out is to love every one that God gives to you, show God's Grace to them and forgive all men their sins, for your Heavenly Father surely has forgiven yours. If you are looking for blessings, it will be at His hand, if looking for acceptance and peace He has already poured it out for you through His cleansing Blood. With His promise of power we can do anything.

And above all things, none of this means anything without Jesus being your Lord and Savior. would I now invite you to bow before Him to pray and believe in your heart that Jesus saves you now from all sins.

"Heavenly Father, have mercy on me. I believe in you and that your word is true. I believe that Jesus Christ is the Son of the living God and that he died on the cross so that I may now have forgiveness for my sins, and have eternal life.

I now believe in my heart that I have received Jesus. Lord, I give you my life and ask you to take full control from this moment on.This I ask the Father in the name of our Lord Jesus Christ."

Amen.

I close this volume with the following quotes from *Francis of Assisi*

"Preach the Gospel at all times and when necessary use words."

"If God can work through me, he can work through anyone."

These pages have been written by Reverend Max L. Manning and dedicated "For the Glory of God."

For inquiries you may contact Reverend Manning at PO Box 161 Topeka, Kansas 66601.

A FINAL TRIBUTE

Max and his Beloved Mary

I want to end this collection of stories with a tribute to my beloved wife of 67 years, Mary Manning. In the preceding chapters I've told just a part of our work together in our Father's vineyard and I trust you've been able to see what a wonderful handmaiden of the Lord she was. She was a talented musician, gifted to play seven different instruments, and she also had a truly lovely voice to sing and speak for our Lord. She provided music for our crusades and church planting for many, many years. A man could not have asked for a more wonderful, a more godly wife. She was truly "a help meet for me" as the Lord God intended for man in the very beginning (Genesis 2:18).

As I'm sure you've noticed, I am writing of Mary in the past tense for she is now with the Lord resting from her labors. On July 7, 2014, just one day short of her 85th birthday, Jesus called her home to her heavenly reward. At exactly 8:55 that morning she laid her cross down and entered into His glorious Kingdom.

As I sat by her bedside that day, we both knew that soon Jesus would be sending His holy angels to escort her through the gates of Glory. Often in the past we had talked about this time, but it had always seemed way off in the future somewhere. On one occasion more recently, I reminded her that when a couple has been married for 67 years as we were that sooner or later one would have to go and one would be left behind. I assured her then that the separation would only be for a short period of time, and in this I now take consolation. I remember asking her, "Honey, if you go ahead of me, will you wait for me at that beautiful gate?" She smiled sweetly and then gently squeezed my hand as if to say, "Of course."

Now the time was swiftly approaching and I sat holding her hand as we gazed at each other, tears streaming from our eyes. As her moment of passage drew closer, Mary's face became more radiant and much more beautiful. I believe she had begun to catch glimpses of another world where Christ was awaiting her arrival. How I wish now that I had photographs of the glorious transformation that was taking place right before my eyes. Her countenance became one of pure joy and a smile spread across her face that could only be matched by one of our angelic counterparts.

I knew she was going, but oh, how I wanted to spend more time — more years! — with my precious darling. We had been together from our youth and it was so difficult to let go, though I knew I had to. Finally I said in my heart, "Yes, Jesus, I release Mary. Please let down the bridge and let her cross over. She will never again have suffering or pain, and someday we will be together again."

As I completed my full surrender, Mary's beautiful brown eyes began to change. No longer was her focus upon me or upon anything of this earth. In that moment, she squeezed my hand, breathed her last breath and then closed her eyes of clay for the final time. As a butterfly that is finally freed of its cocoon, she had taken flight, leaving her temporal dwelling behind to await the resurrection of the righteous. Oh, how glorious are the promises of God!

Before she left, I promised Mary that I would continue on with the work of the Lord until it was time for me to join her in our heavenly home. At the time of this writing I am 86 years of age and still serving our Lord Jesus Christ with all the strength He gives me. Yet today I carry a burden for the less fortunate, still traveling often to help relieve their suffering and to win souls into the Kingdom. As the Lord enables me, I intend to do so until He says it is enough and bids me, "Welcome home." I know Mary will be right there by His side to greet me, too.

CPSIA information can be obtained at www.ICGtesting.com
Printed in the USA
LVOW07s0300220415

435558LV00001B/27/P

9 781498 425933